DESIGN AND DETAIL

DESIGN AND DETAIL

THE PRACTICAL GUIDE TO STYLING A HOUSE

.

TRICIA GUILD

TEXT BY TRICIA GUILD AND ELIZABETH WILHIDE

.

PHOTOGRAPHY BY DAVID MONTGOMERY

CONRAN OCTOPUS

FOR RICHARD AND LISA

ART EDITOR **MERYL LLOYD**

ILLUSTRATOR **SARAH JOHN**

PROJECT EDITOR **JOANNA BRADSHAW**

EDITOR AND CONTRIBUTOR **DIANA MANSOUR**

EDITORIAL ASSISTANT **SIMON WILLIS**

PICTURE RESEARCHER **NADINE BAZAR**

PRODUCTION **SHANE LASK**

■

First published in 1988 by Conran Octopus Limited
37 Shelton Street, London WC2H 9HN

This paperback edition published in 1993 by
Conran Octopus Limited

Reprinted 1995

British Library Cataloguing in Publication Data
Guild, Tricia
    Design and detail: the practical guide
    to styling a house
    1. Residences. Interior design – Amateurs' manuals
I. Title
747
                    ISBN 1-85029-801-7

Typeset by Servis Filmsetting Limited
Printed in Hong Kong

CONTENTS

INTRODUCTION

The first moment I saw our new garden, one of the changes I decided to make was to add a pond. One day, when most of the work had been completed, my mother came to visit. She pointed out that what I had designed and built was a perfect replica (but on a smaller scale) of the beautiful pond that used to be in my grandfather's garden years ago. I realized that it was quite true; somehow the memory had remained with me all that time, a lasting inspiration.

The whole process of design can at times be quite mysterious; it is certainly hard to define. Design, style – whatever you choose to call it – arises out of feeling, an intuition for colour, scale and pattern. The substantial part of my working life is spent with designs, developing fabrics, wallcoverings and furnishings. For this to be rewarding the result must be functional, practical, stylish and innovative.

I believe it is important for a designer to be firmly in touch with the way in which products are really used. For me this means an ongoing involvement in interior decoration, which is both challenging and a constant stimulus for new ideas. This book is about some of my own interior design concepts.

INSPIRATION

Nature has always been the key to my work as a designer. First of all, it provides a direct inspiration, suggesting ideas for colour, pattern and form. But nature means more to me than a convenient source of ideas: it is a central thought in my whole philosophy of design. Flowers are neither an afterthought nor a detail, they are a truly positive element in an interior. They bring vitality, spontaneity, and a sense of change; they make people feel welcome. Their value is more to do with the effort they require – the daily watering and rearranging – than with any material worth.

The freedom and fluidity of flowers are qualities that I try to capture in fabric. Flowers are always changing, from moment to moment – opening out, evolving, and eventually browning and shedding petals. The Japanese recognize the beauty of this process, and for them the peak of perfection comes just as the edges of a chrysanthemum's petals begin to brown. Or think of the way parrot tulips look just before they drop.

And, of course, plants and flowers link interiors to the outside world, not just by adding a living presence but by reflecting changing seasons and patterns of growth. Large-scale commercial gardening means that hothouse versions of many flowers can be bought all the year round, but there is something much more satisfying about choosing flowers that are right for the season as well as the place.

Nature as a whole is enormously inspiring – the sculptural forms of trees and foliage, the rich patterns inherent in different landscapes and the strong, structural quality of traditional formal gardens.

One of England's most famous gardens, Sissinghurst, which was begun by Vita Sackville-West in 1930, has been a constant source of inspiration to me, as it has to so many others. The White Garden and the use of striking colour contrasts make this a place I like to visit again and again. There is also the work

Above left The variety and colour of landscapes provide a rich source of inspiration.

Centre left Flowers constantly change shape and appearance, lending life and vitality to any interior.

Below left Different styles of architecture can lead us to discover new forms and ideas.

of the great Victorian gardener Gertrude Jekyll, who has had a lasting influence on our notions of garden design. Many old gardens have an architectural quality, with walled 'rooms', hedges and archways creating a graphic framework and a strength of line that allows the planting to be free.

A sense of place has often been another important element in the work of artists and designers. Gauguin found inspiration in Tahiti, Matisse in the south of France, Hockney in the suburbs of Los Angeles. Different cultures, different land-scapes and different qualities of light can provide a jolt to the senses which increases awareness and stimulates creativity. But it is not necessary to travel on a grand scale to strange, exotic locations; the same kind of experience can be found closer to home by visiting exhibitions at museums and galleries and by reading books on art, culture and history.

It is often difficult to work backwards and uncover the reasons and impulses – the inspiration – that move us in one particular direction rather than another. It took a chance comment of my mother's, for example, to make me realize that what I thought was a conscious design solution was in fact a treasured memory of a beautiful place. What I have sketched out here are just my own starting points: you will have to discover your own. Travel, works of art, the wealth of historical styles of decoration, and architecture – all of these can open our eyes and make us see things in a fresh light.

Keep a scrapbook of ideas – postcards of favourite places, gardens or paintings; magazine cuttings of interiors that appeal; even snips of fabric and pieces of ribbon or braid. The aim should be to arrive at a style of your own; an expression of your particular tastes and experiences. I'm not suggesting that you embark on an arduous programme of research – just practise observing patterns, colours and shapes. And, above all, trust your own instinctive feelings and preferences.

Above right Travel, and the experience of foreign cultures, offer an important stimulus to the imagination.

Centre right Architectural details provide a neat finishing touch, and are worth a careful examination.

Below right The inspiration I gain from nature is central to my whole philosophy of design.

ELEMENTS OF DESIGN

There can never be a rulebook for design. Because good design to a large extent springs from a combination of enthusiasm and flair, it is in one sense unpredictable, and any principles or rules you might devise would soon be broken in the creative search for originality. The hardest part about design is keeping it all alive – it is this spirit that is so difficult to analyze or pin down. Nevertheless, I think it is possible to say that there are several important elements which are always present in the best work. The first is confidence with colour; the second is attention to detail; and the last, but perhaps the most crucial, is a sense of wit or humour.

COLOUR

Colour is an element that tends to inspire a degree of fear. In a sense this is quite right, because colour has an influence on the quality of life above and beyond other considerations so that, faced with a choice, many people find themselves unable to come to a decision. Of course reactions to different colours and shades of colours vary widely, which makes it impossible to generalize.

The most important point about colour is that it is relative – our appreciation of a particular shade depends to a large extent on the colours nearby, the setting and the views beyond. A greeny blue, for example, might look cold on its own, but considerably warmer next to a pink. And the outside world – a city view, a seascape, a country garden – will also affect our perceptions. Colours cannot be taken out of context.

Aside from the type of confidence that can be built up by studying nature, works of art and other inspirational examples, familiarity with colour can be gained by practical experiment. Sampling different colours – that is, actually painting patches on the wall or assembling swatches of fabric – will enable you to understand the inherent vitality of colour combinations. Here the crucial factor to remember is to sample colours in proportion. If you think you might like to cover a cushion in salmon pink, with bright green piping as trimming, make sure that the pink swatch is proportionately larger than the green swatch. Faced with equal-sized pieces of pink and green, most people would abandon the idea of placing such strong colours together, but it is just this kind of audacious mix that brings an interior to life. Learning about colour often involves first deciding what *you* like. To which colours are you instinctively drawn? Which colours repel you? Are you in the habit of choosing colours for your home because they are 'safe' and uncontroversial or do you have a more positive reaction to them?

When I am developing ideas for interiors, I usually start with a favourite colour and build on that by assembling a family of shades that work with it. Then I look at contrasts. You can try the same exercise yourself – but try to avoid using tiny colour cards or minute squares of fabric. To get a reasonably accurate impression of the final result you have to view the colours in large enough samples – and by different types of light, both natural and artificial.

DETAILS

Another aspect of the interior where it is important to take infinite pains is details – everything from light switches to cupboard handles. Unlike colour, people don't find details frightening, they find them boring. As a result, this element tends to be neglected, skimped and generally glossed over; but if colour expresses the whole spirit and life of a scheme, details are its underpinning.

Details should not be obvious, but they should be right. They create a hidden vitality, if you like, establishing relationships between different objects, modulating the effect of competing centres of attention, introducing a sense of rhythm, and strengthening line. In our house, for example, I decided that all the 'functional' details should be black – light switches and fittings, power points, door handles and hinges. The effect of this disciplined coordination is to provide a graphic base for the strong colours used on the walls and the rich patterns of the soft furnishings. In the same way, the use of piping on cushions and seat covers, edgings on blinds and binding on fabric-covered walls gives a crisp, clean line. By using contrasting colours – or patterns – for these details, you immediately set up a relationship between different patterns and surfaces that has a rhythm all of its own. Of course, paying attention to details takes time and trouble – I was unable to find black hinges or switches in the design I wanted so I had to have them sprayed black – but the results are invariably worthwhile.

But even the greatest skill with colour, or the most careful choice of accessories and trimmings, may not prevent the result from looking flat and lifeless. This is why I think that a sense of humour is such an important part of good design. Humour, flair, surprise – these are all ways of describing the happy accident, the odd combination of objects or the quirky touch which makes a room a living interior rather than a studio set.

DESIGN IN CONTEXT

How to translate inspiration into practice is one of the challenges of design. Designers Guild collections are based on a wide spectrum of ideas of which nature is a facet, but along with many other rich sources of inspiration.

Flowers have often been a theme of Designers Guild prints, from the stylized Indian gibweed motifs of the first collection, to the painterly Hodgkin tulip or the figurative chintz that, as the names *Hollyhocks*, *Wild Roses*, *Lilac* and *Paper Roses* suggest, seek to evoke the splendour of a flowering garden. Specifically, collections such as *Anemone*, *Ornamental Garden* and *Maypole* derive from an interest in flower forms and their various colours.

Other designs evoke a sense of place. The first Designers Guild collection, *Village*, was based on Indian motifs and consisted of a group of fabrics patterned with small designs that could be mixed together – this represented something of a breakthrough at the time. More recently, Italy has been an important influence. Palladian villas, notably Malcontenta with its breathtaking *trompe-l'oeil* decorations by Veronese; vivid Italian handwoven silk brocades and damasks; the cheerful, almost primitive motifs of Italian ceramics; Venetian marbled paper; and the wonderful depth and texture of frescoed walls have provided a whole collage of exciting ideas for

new collections, most notably *Grandiflora* and *Gesso*.

There are also strong connections with artists working in other areas of the decorative arts. The textile and knitwear designer Kaffe Fassett created a collection called *Geraniums*, initially inspired by one of his superb collages. The *Waterleaf* collection arose from a collaboration with the ceramicist Janice Tchalenko. And a group of fabrics with bold leaf and flower shapes was created specially for Designers Guild by the painter Howard Hodgkin.

Ideas can also be gleaned from the past. Old fabrics and old documents are a constant source of ideas which can be translated into the more contemporary forms that relate specifically to the work of Designers Guild.

However the inspiration for a design is conceived, the application must be in a practical context. The guiding philosophy of Designers Guild has always been to relate fabric or wallpaper patterns to the way in which they will eventually be used in a room.

In interior decoration, fabrics or wallpapers are just one element of the design process. The combination of different fabrics and colours, the setting, shape, proportion and positioning of the furniture are just a few of the other areas that are fundamental to achieving the final result.

DESIGNING PATTERNS

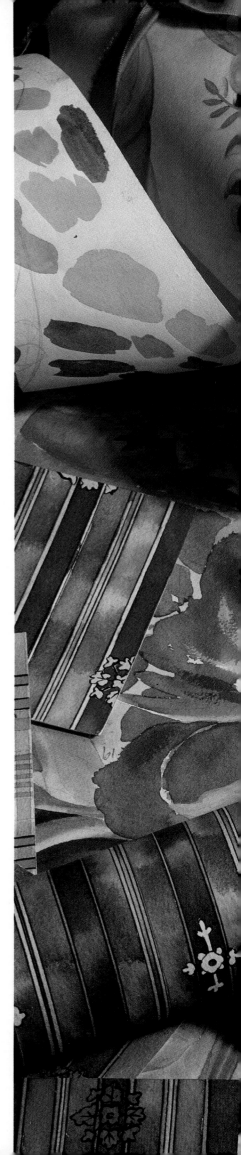

Pattern is all about rhythm. The scale of the image or motif, the way it repeats across a background, the nature of the background – plain, patterned or textured – the balance of colours; all of these elements have to work together in an harmonious whole. If they do, the pattern will flow and come to life; if they don't, it will look flat or confused.

Pattern design often starts with an idea for a motif. When you look at an object – a vase, say – you usually see it flat, as a picture or a painting. In pattern design the object has to be translated into a repeat, duplicated against a background.

This basic relationship between image and background can then be modified in all types of subtle ways. Often, a strong image will not work with a flat background. For example, one of our recent designs, *Fiorita*, combines two apparent opposites – a freely-drawn pattern of lilacs and a contrasting pattern of stripes. In this pattern the fluidity of the flowers is given strength and depth by the geometric element. Another example from the same collection, *Giardino*, consists of large, simple garden flowers. In this case I wanted a quality of tonal gradation to give the pattern a slightly traditional look, so we printed it on cotton damask, a heavy, textured surface that supplies that extra dimension. For detailed designs, I use glazed cotton.

In our work at Designers Guild, where the quality of colours and colour relationships is all-important, we invariably design in watercolour on a white background, aiming for a painterly quality, or the clear transparency you see when light shines through leaves and petals. Needless to say, in the process of creating a fabric or wallpaper, adjustments are always necessary. Because of the production processes involved, it is often only when the printing machines are rolling that it is possible to see precisely what alterations must be made – changes to the weight or tone of a particular shade that will affect the whole balance of a print. *Grandiflora*, a busy, intricate print, needed just this type of adjustment. Originally one of the flowers in the design was a strong, rich red, a colour which drew too much attention to itself and upset the tonal balance. When this was changed to a softer rose, it was intense enough to stand up to the blues in the print, but the colours were no longer fighting each other.

As in interiors, the quality of a pattern can be greatly affected by details. To achieve a sense of depth and vitality, we use between twelve and eighteen different colours for most of our designs. *Spirale*, for example, includes four different greys, each one subtly distinct from the others. Even background stripes are printed in two shades.

DEVELOPMENT OF A STYLE

Design ideas, even fabric or wallpaper patterns, are irrelevant unless they work in practice, in the context in which you want to use them. The purpose of this book is to show a setting in which all the elements work together so that you can extract ideas and go on to apply them in your own home.

I have always used the place I live in as a setting in which my ideas are conceived and applied – not as a showcase for finished designs but as the context in which the ideas are generated. It is a personal way of working, but it is close to what most people experience.

The house that we show in the following pages was designed and decorated in this way, but I do not expect it to remain the same for long. Wherever I live I keep changing things – there is nothing more

lifeless than the 'perfect' result, which is painstakingly designed in every detail and then tended, unaltered for years, like a museum exhibit.

Our previous home went through two major incarnations. Like our present home, it was a mid-Victorian terraced house in London, similar to the latter in architectural style but smaller in scale. To begin with, in the early days of Designers Guild, the house was tumbling with patterns, including Kaffe Fassett's *Geranium* designs. The overall look of the decorative scheme was very nostalgic, with cane furniture, 1930s ceramics and a pine kitchen. When I redecorated, it was simpler, less nostalgic but still soft, with pastel colours creating a base for my collection of ceramics. Again, the theme was essentially floral and countrified. In

the main bedroom a cabbage rose print was the coordinating element that linked the wallpaper, the four-poster bed hangings and the Roman blinds. It is interesting to note those design elements that are carried through to the present house; namely the padded stool at the bottom of the bed, the sumptuous cushions and the strong fabric pattern.

Above A soft country look in my previous house. The scheme is unified by the use of pastels, light pinks and greens.

Above right The same room, in a later incarnation. Pastels have given way to a natural, monochrome scheme.

Right A detail of the living room, showing 'structural' shelving built into an alcove.

Far right A pale blue cabbage rose print was the basis of the decorative scheme.

A NEW STYLE FOR AN OLD HOUSE

Above and right The front elevation of the house retains a strong Victorian character, with architectural details typical of the period and style of the house. Any fundamental change would have destroyed the unity of the terrace.

The present house represents a dramatic change of mood. Like the previous house, it has a traditional quality, both in the character of the architectural details and in the proportions and disposition of the spaces. But here, rather than allow the period style of the house to influence the decoration as previously, I wanted to achieve a more contemporary and graphic look, with strong colours creating the basis for different atmospheres throughout the house. At the same time,

I wanted to keep the integrity of the house intact, blending old and new in a sympathetic fashion rather than superimposing one on the other. In fact, much of the effort involved in the initial design was directed at maintaining this balance and harmony.

Although this book is about style and decoration, the basic shell – the architecture, the proportions of a house, its scale and layout – will affect how the interior style works. Before you start to decorate

it is important to consider first whether you need to improve the spatial quality of your house.

In my case, I spent a year converting and extending the house to get the framework right. Working with Philip Geraghty, who coordinated the building project, we designed an extension at the back of the building, reorganized the layout of the first floor, and removed some partition walls on the ground floor and in the basement.

Large-scale alterations such as these require careful planning. Especially if you are creating a new area from two existing ones, rather than restoring an original layout, you will have to consider how the change will affect the scale and proportion of the space. These architectural relationships are fundamental when planning a new interior and must be worked out in detail on paper. Only when the layouts are absolutely right should building work begin.

Above and left From the rear, a new extension provided the opportunity to create new architectural detailing. A grey metal staircase and balustrading link the French windows on the living room level with the garden.

In conjunction with the structural work, it is necessary to plan changes to services — electricity, plumbing, lighting and heating. And at this stage it is best to have some idea of how the furniture will be arranged since this will affect the location of power points and light fittings.

Structural alterations or major conversions also affect detailing. Taking care over details — especially at those points where old meets new — is the best way to integrate different styles of building. I liked the aged quality of the cornices and ceiling mouldings and wanted to keep them. For the same reason, I did not have all the walls replastered — only where it was really necessary. Living in the house as it was changing, I was beginning to have some idea of the way in which the colours and patterns would eventually work and I decided that, in order to provide a consistency that would cut through the richness of the decoration, there would be modern door furniture, switches, points and light fittings, and that all of these would be black.

But I also devised a new architectural motif which became a theme running throughout the entire house. This recurrent detail — four squares arranged within a square — was inspired by a graphic idea found in the work of Charles Rennie Mackintosh, the famous Scottish architect and designer who worked at the turn of the century. It occurs in the new windows at the back of the house, the bathroom grilles, the radiator ducts, the door architraves, the handles inset in the kitchen cabinets and the painted floor decoration in the morning room, sounding a contemporary but classical note throughout.

Clockwise from top right Matt black power socket; square detail on shelf support; black wall-mounted uplighter; square inset cupboard handles; rag rugs woven from fabrics used in the house; floor-standing uplighter.
Far right Cotton and silk throws by Richard Womersley.

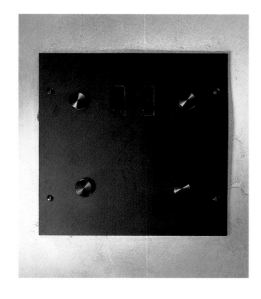

CONTEMPORARY STYLING

THE HALL
AND
STAIRS

Where do you begin? The prospect of decorating an entire house fills many people with panic.

It is easy to forget that you already possess some of the information you need. Imagine a situation where you had to go out and replace your clothes' wardrobe tomorrow. You would not need to visit every shop in the high street before deciding what to buy, since the tastes and preferences you had already would affect your choice. It is just the same with decoration. Once you consider your own practical needs along with the ideas you already have, a scheme will emerge.

When decorating an entire house, think of it as a totality, a series of spaces linked together. Because rooms are physically connected by halls and stairways, they should display common themes and styles. This is not to say that they should all be the same, but they should work together and complement each other to strengthen the whole composition. Equally, the hall, because it links the house together, should both sum up the decorative theme and hint at what is to come.

■■

DESIGNING A HALL

Too often, the hall is a bland, neutral space that creates no impression of its own. Hallways tend to be neglected because they are rarely wide enough to accommodate very much furniture and, especially in terraced houses, they are often dark and lack natural light. But the hall provides both an introduction and a welcome to your house, and it is vital to treat it as a positive space to be decorated with care.

Sometimes structural changes can vastly improve a hall's spatial qualities. In our house there was originally a small bathroom at the top of the first flight of stairs, directly off the landing. When designing the new extension, I decided to open up this area and light the space with a skylight. The impact on the hall was immediate – a glimpse of light coming from above created a sense of openness in place of what had been a dead end. To maintain this feeling, it was decided not to enclose the area with a dividing wall.

Other structural changes can also alter the way a hall works and the impression it gives. Blocking up redundant doorways can simplify routes from room to room; widening or adding entrances can create a sense of drama.

VIEWS AND DETAILS

Halls are all about views. In our house, with its central theme of strong colour, it was important to make sure that the sequence of colours worked throughout. But there are other ways of creating views and vistas. The hall is an important place in the house for displaying flowers, which add vitality and freshness, reinforcing that sense of welcome. If there is room, the entrance is also a good place for a table, where favourite objects can be arranged. The hall table is necessarily very narrow – like a console or shelf; it provides a strip of bright colour that makes a striking contrast with the walls. Together with the pattern made by objects arranged on the table top, this gives a flavour of what is to come.

Mirrors reflect other rooms and maximize light, and areas of wall can be hung with pictures, generating interest and vitality: if you arrange pictures on each level they will lead the eye up through the house.

In the hall, architectural details are more apparent than anywhere else. Doors leading to other rooms, stairs, balustrades and handrails, skirting boards, cornices – all are thrown into relief simply because there is rarely very much else to distract the eye. Nothing gives a house greater unity than consistency in details, and care exercised here promotes a real feeling of quality.

Well before colours were selected for use in the house, the decision was made that all light fittings, door furniture, handles, switches and sockets would be black. This, as mentioned before, was designed to produce a contemporary, graphic quality and balance out the richness of pattern and colour. At the same time, all the ceilings and cornices would be white, again as a foil for the strong colours, but also as a crisp, understated treatment for the original architectural details, helping old blend with new.

The position of new details such as switches is just as important as their colour. The standard arrangement is to place the light switch well up on the wall, theoretically for safety reasons, to keep it out of a child's reach (although sockets, potentially much more dangerous, are generally sited close to the floor). I prefer switches at a much lower height, aligned with the door handle, so that when you enter a dark room there is no fumbling to turn on the light – the switch is there at hand-level. As well as this practical advantage, having switches, handles, thermostats and hi-fi controls all at the same level gives a much cleaner line.

It was less obvious how to treat the woodwork, particularly as there were two types, the original and the new, to reconcile. First it was decided that all the window frames and the new woodwork would be white whereas the original doors would be given a colour. Black was rejected because it might be too oppressive. Then I considered painting the doors charcoal and adding a grained finish. However, when the walls were painted they had great depth and character, and the introduction of another paint finish would have looked contrived and overdone. Eventually a warm blue grey was chosen for the original doors and skirting boards – more interesting than black and less intrusive than a special finish.

FLOORS

Hall floors receive a lot of attention, as well as a great deal of wear. I prefer the traditional solution of a hard floor in the entrance because it is practical and easy to maintain. A certain amount of dust and dirt will inevitably get tracked in from outside and it is pointless to waste energy worrying about a precious floor covering. Even so, it is still a good idea to provide a large place to wipe feet. One solution is to stop the flooring short of the door and make a generous well, the width of the hall, which can be filled with a sturdy coir mat.

The original Edwardian hall floor in the house – consisting of black and white tiles – was unfortunately in too poor a condition to be restored. But when we removed layers of linoleum from the stairs to the basement we discovered beautiful and sound stone steps. Inspired by the discovery, we decided to lay stone in the hall, choosing big oblong slabs for a rather contemporary look and a warm but neutral colour to promote a sense of tranquillity.

Right The hall view. Details are important – the mahogany handrail, for example, is painted black rather than the grey of the skirting boards to give a crisp, strong line.

SEQUENCE OF COLOURS

Even if you do not intend to decorate the whole house straight away, it is good practice to draw up a paint schedule for each room, listing the colours you want to use and where – ceilings, walls or woodwork. This forces you to devise a scheme that works as a whole, rather than a piecemeal room-by-room solution. Colour boards (see page 41) are also useful and help you to adjust the tones of different shades so that the transitions are harmonious. For example, the original colour chosen for the terracotta bedroom was rather pale. When we looked at it in the context of the colours of the other rooms, it was obvious that it had to be stronger and deeper.

The sequence of colours in the house started with the idea of using a particular green in the sitting room. Once blue had been chosen for the hall, creating a dramatic contrast of strong colours, the idea of using blocks of colour throughout the house suggested itself as a natural development.

There are many myths about colour. One is that strong shades such as blue and green clash and should never be used together. While certain tones unquestionably do jar and are uncomfortable in combination, others are very accommodating. Both blue and green, perhaps because they occur universally in nature – sky and water, grass and trees – can always live happily with other colours. The decision to paint the hall blue created the opportunity to make exciting and varied transitions from room to room.

Another myth is that blue is a cold colour, to be shunned in interior decoration, but this is not the case. The long tradition of the use of blue in the decorative arts, notably in ceramics, shows how the colour has been used and enjoyed for centuries.

Once the colours of the hall and living room had been established, I decided that the morning room should be a warm pink to avoid repeating the blue of the landing, and then

The
Hall
—
Cornflower
Blue

The
Living
Room
—
Bright
Jade

The
Master
Bedroom
—
Fresh
Mint
Green

The
Attic
Study
—
Leaf
Green

that the ground-floor study should be yellow. At first I intended that this should be an upholstered room, with pattern on the walls, but the glimpse of yellow at the end of the hall proved to be an important part of the way the hall works.

Mixing strong colours sounds like a recipe for creating a hectic environment, with every surface competing for attention. In fact, the reverse happens. Although all the colours are intense, there is continuity in the style and depth of the finish. The strength of all these colours balances out and paradoxically promotes a sense of calm.

The painted finish is itself an important consideration. Once fabrics for the sitting room were assembled, I knew that flat colour would not stand up to the rich patterns of the fabrics. And, although I wanted a textured, layered look for the paintwork, I did not want the result to look like a paint technique – something unavoidable if you opt for a finish that

is defined by the method of achieving it. Sponged, ragged or stippled walls inevitably bear the imprint of the tool used to create the effect. It is better to decide how you want the finish to look; many different methods may be needed to build up to the final appearance.

After seeing the Palladian villa Malcontenta, with its wealth of painted decoration, I knew that the walls should have the luminous but faded colour of Italian fresco and should suggest the depth and texture of painted plaster. To achieve this look I searched through books for reference; colours were selected as a base for the finished tones; sample boards were made to test the relationships between the colours.

Without question, executing a special finish on this scale is a professional job. If you are skilled and patient, you may be successful in tackling a small area, but experience is needed to create an effect over an expanse of wall.

The Morning Room
—
Rosy pink

The Study
—
Lemon yellow

The Terra-Cotta Bedroom
—
Warm terra-cotta

Kitchen and Dining room
—
Plaster pink

THE PAINTED WALLS

In a traditional fresco, powdered pigments are first mixed in water and then applied to wet plaster so that the colour sinks into the wall. Add a century of wear and tear and you arrive at the luminous, well-worn effect that I wanted to achieve in my hall. To create this beautifully aged texture using ordinary paints (emulsion in this case) on existing plaster, it is necessary to paint several layers of closely related tones in such a way that a little of the previous layers shows through at each stage.

The base coat used in my hall was a soft blue, into which different tints of crimson and/or ultramarine were blended for the successive coats to produce the blue textured finish.

Special paint finishes call for patience and skill, but the method used here should be within your scope as long as you are prepared to experiment with colours and practice the techniques repeatedly before starting in earnest. The most important requirement is the ability to work consistently and evenly, not just over small areas, but over whole walls.

PAINTING THE WALLS

Prepare the walls for painting in the usual way by filling cracks, sanding and washing. Choose a base colour for the wall; this should be a softer, lighter tone of the final colour that you are aiming for. Take a can of pure white emulsion paint and decant small quantities of it into five or six containers. To each container of pure white blend in a different tint of the base colour so that you have a range of shades; if you need to thin the paint, add a little water.

Paint and number a small square of each colour on the wall and keep records of how each tint was created in case you need to mix repeat blends.

Apply the base coat smoothly and evenly to the walls until you have what appears to be a finished, painted wall.

Next, apply from four to six more coats of paint (using a different tint for each coat). Allow the paint to dry thoroughly between layers. Take a small amount of paint on the end of the brush and drag it very softly over the surface; if the brush becomes clogged with paint, carefully remove the excess.

Each different colour tint should be applied in such a way that flecks and traces of the previous colours show through. If any stray paint marks appear, wipe them away immediately and, if necessary, retouch the affected areas when the painting is finished.

The aim of this technique is to produce an impression of colour and depth rather than a formal finish which looks like a museum piece, so there is no need for a final coat of varnish. The walls can be washed carefully when necessary, and any area that gets badly marked can be retouched quite easily, which means that the finish is just as practical as more conventional paintwork but its overall effect is much more interesting and original.

THE LIVING ROOM

The living room is the heart of the house. It is the place to bring friends, entertain and relax. Unlike the starched formality of Victorian parlours the living room today functions as the centre of family life and may have to accommodate a diverse range of interests and activities.

Whatever the size of the room, space must be organized carefully to provide distinct areas for different uses, but at the same time remain an harmonious whole. Planning is essential, and in a sense you are obliged to finish the room before you can start it; this does not mean that you have to buy everything at once, but you should have a clear picture of the end result in your mind.

What makes a living room come to life – a place to which people gravitate rather than a too-perfect showcase – is the personal atmosphere. Here you can surround yourself with favourite things. Whether it is a painting or a beautiful bowl, by displaying it, you add a narrative dimension and invite other people to enjoy it along with you.

PLANNING THE LAYOUT

With a layout common to many older terraced houses, the first floor of our house originally consisted of two reception rooms; one facing the street, the other facing the garden. To make an area big enough for entertaining and to create a sense of space, I decided to take down the dividing wall and make one living room running from the front of the house to the back. One advantage of this alteration is that it provided a natural break which could be exploited to make the space work for different uses. But there were also disadvantages – the chief of these being an inbuilt symmetry that restricted options for layout. The new room contained two fireplaces lined up along the same wall, one for each half, and because fireplaces are natural focal points for seating arrangements, this meant that both halves of the room would have to be set out in virtually the same way. To avoid this problem, I decided to remove the fireplace from the garden end of the room.

The living room also had two entrances, one on either side of the original divide. Since the room was to be used as a whole, only one doorway was necessary. Blocking up the door in the end of the room that faced the street provided more wall space where a large painting could be hung, giving this area more of an enclosed feeling.

The furniture layout evolved as a consequence of these changes, defined the theme of two spaces and determined the route of traffic through them. At the street end of the room, furniture is

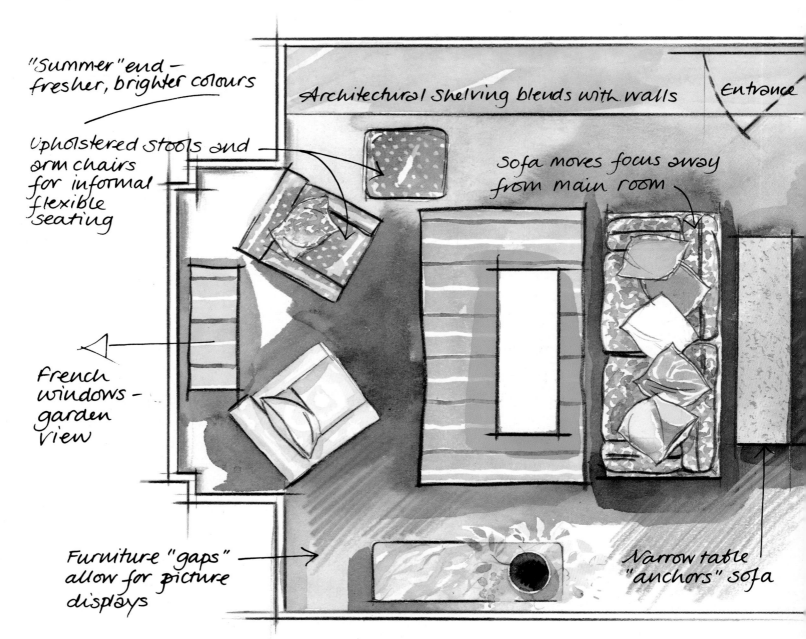

"Summer" end –
fresher, brighter colours

Architectural shelving blends with walls

Entrance

Upholstered stools and
arm chairs
for informal
flexible
seating

sofa moves focus away
from main room

French
windows –
garden
view

Furniture "gaps"
allow for picture
displays

Narrow table
"anchors" sofa

grouped around the hearth, with a large sofa directly facing the fire. I saw this part of the living room as the 'winter' end, a place for entertaining. In the other area, where the fireplace was removed, I positioned a sofa to face the French windows and overlook the garden. This became the 'summer' end, and the bookshelves that line one wall lend it a more private, contemplative atmosphere, making it a place for reading or listening to music. Here, a console table placed against the back of the sofa provides a

space for objects and visually anchors the sofa's position, acting rather like a wall or room divider in this respect.

Furniture layout should always include an element of flexibility. Inevitably there will be fixed points in any arrangement: once you have determined the position of the sofa and accompanying chairs, these will form the basis of the layout. But to keep the room alive it is a good idea to incorporate smaller pieces that can be easily moved from place to place as need dictates.

The main conversation area in most living rooms typically includes a coffee table, a piece of furniture which has become indispensable. While there is no doubt that the coffee table is a very useful place for magazines, trays, drinks and so on, many of the available designs contribute little to the style of a room. A large table at low level can also impose a certain rigidity on the layout. One solution, if, like me, you cannot find a coffee table you like, is to use a pair of small tables together.

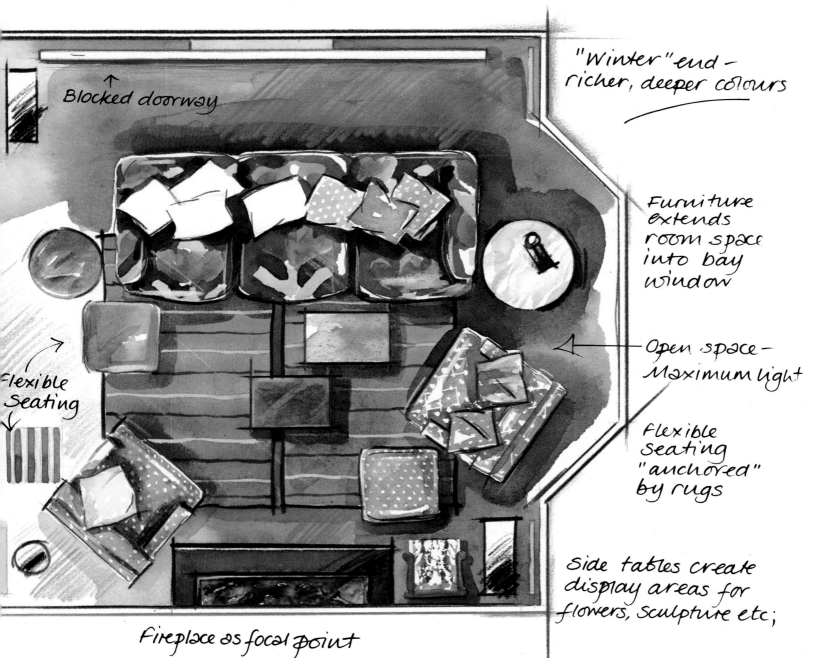

Blocked doorway

"Winter" end – richer, deeper colours

Furniture extends room space into bay window

Open space – Maximum light

Flexible Seating

Flexible seating "anchored" by rugs

Side tables create display areas for flowers, sculpture etc;

Fireplace as focal point

DESIGNING A ROOM

Lack of planning is as serious a handicap as a lack of imagination. Work out all your ideas on paper first: even if you have to tear up several schemes before you find the right solution, you will always save time and money.

The first step is to take accurate measurements of the room and transfer them to paper – graph paper will help you keep dimensions in scale. Mark the position of doors, windows, fireplaces, existing radiators, switches, sockets and light fittings. Then, working to the same scale, cut out shapes of the furniture which you own or intend to buy and move the pieces about on the plan to try out different arrangements. You can colour in the cut-outs if you know which fabrics you will be using for upholstery.

Use the plan to establish the level of change that is required. The plan may confirm that a new furniture layout is all you need; it may show you where extra sockets should go, or it may demonstrate that you could block up an under-used doorway or take down a wall to improve the quality of the space. If you are designing a room completely from scratch, a plan will help you to integrate services, lighting and layout and to arrange access and circulation – the flow of traffic – from area to area.

THE COLOUR BOARD

Another important tool in the planning process is the colour board. Professional interior designers and decorators use colour boards or 'scheme' boards to present proposals to clients; equally, you can make your own colour board to see how your ideas are developing.

A colour board is nothing more exotic than a single sheet of card or paper to which you attach samples of the colours and patterns you intend to use in the room. What is important to remember is that your samples of colours and fabrics should be in proportion. If you wish to cover a sofa with a red and white print, and to trim it with green piping, put the main fabric swatch together with a smaller scrap of green. It is impossible to judge the effect of a contrasting trim if both samples are of equal size.

Aside from suggesting ideas for trimming, colour boards help you to check that the colour you have chosen to paint the walls really does pick up that particular shade in the chair fabric; or that the palette of contrasting colours and patterns that you intend to use for cushion covers is effective against the background of the sofa upholstery. And, if you assemble colour boards for the whole house, you can work out how to perpetuate certain themes, colours or patterns from room to room.

The same colours or patterns appearing in different rooms in different applications introduce a level of harmony and a rhythm that is difficult to achieve if you consider each room in isolation. In our house, for example, the green of the painted floor in the morning room echoes the green walls of the master bedroom; the yellow walls in my husband's study relate to the colour of the armchair near the window in the living room.

"Summer" end —

"winter" end —

Rag rugs woven
from fabrics in
the room

Coral silk
Brocade

— Black coir flooring

Hodgkin Sofa
fabric — "Moss"

Moss green
for upholstered
stool and
cushions

Cushion
combinations —
Jade / black
Coral / green
Moss / blue

Lilac striped
silk on stool

yellow silk
on chair
and
stool

Hodgkin
glazed
cotton
for
sofa

← Jade green
painted walls

Brocades
for cushions

THE DECORATIVE SCHEME

Pattern, colour and texture are the raw ingredients of decoration: in practice, there is often one particular fabric, rug or painting which forms the basis of a scheme and determines the way it evolves. In the case of the living room, my starting point was the flower fabric designed by Howard Hodgkin, that had already been chosen to cover the large sofa in the 'winter' end of the room.

This fabric, with its large-scale, almost abstract pattern of blue flowers on a black background, could easily have dominated everything else. Original and intensely coloured, it imposed demands of its own. Because the fabric is so strong, simple coordination – picking out plain colours from the design to use elsewhere in the room – would have been less interesting. I also rejected the idea of keeping the rest of the room simple and monochromatic in order to focus attention on the Hodgkin design. Instead, the approach I chose was to match the strength of the fabric with other intense colours and patterns; some clashing, some coordinating. Within this context, the fabric retains its impact, but also becomes more of an integral part of the rest of the decoration. For the sofa at the 'summer' end of the living room I chose another, quite different Hodgkin fabric – a pink, white and green print, with a light, vibrant texture. This print was also used to edge the plain white Roman blinds at both ends of the room.

With these two Hodgkin fabrics as the basis for creating the different atmospheres of the two seating areas, I then chose other fabrics for cushions, chairs and stools, repeated throughout the room to pull the entire scheme together. These were beautiful French and Italian silks and brocades, with great depth and intensity – a green fabric patterned with bees which is used to cover two armchairs, one in each area, and a subtle

Left The 'garden' end of the living room has been arranged to make the most of the view from the French windows.

brocade in pinks and yellows. The green of the bee fabric is precisely the same green as the leaf in the Hodgkin flower print; the brocade is a contrast in mood and colour. But an important part of the way the room works is the injection of a small amount of bright yellow, used to cover an armchair in the 'summer' end, a colour which is repeated only in the tray set on the table in front of the chair.

It is always important to know where to stop. A vivid combination of colours and patterns requires a plain background to allow the scheme to breathe. It was equally important to retain a contemporary atmosphere and to avoid over-upholstering the room. For these reasons, the plain and functional light fittings are black metal; the windows are covered with tailored white Roman blinds, connected to the sofa furnishings by their print edging. And on the floor there is black coir. Coir provides both a good base for rugs and an interesting texture of its own. It is warmer and more giving than a hard floor for a house in a cool climate, but has a crisper, more graphic quality than carpet. Previously I had always used natural coir but on this occasion a neutral colour would not have been strong enough.

Although much of the furniture in the living room is upholstered, there are also antique wooden pieces, such as the round Biedermeier sewing table and the marble-topped chest of drawers. These mediate between plain and patterned surfaces and give the room a sense of depth by acting as a reminder of the past.

Just as important as knowing how to put colours and patterns together is the combination of textures. Texture affects the way in which colour is perceived and gives depth to pattern.

In the living room, as well as the contrasts between silk, silk damask and brocade, cotton twill and glazed cotton upholstery, there are also the more forthright textures of wool and chenille blankets and cotton rag rugs.

ARRANGING OBJECTS

Above Shelves and tabletops carry collections of flowers, ceramics and books – frequently changed for variety and vitality. *Right* Torso sculpture by Glynn Williams.

Everything that is visible is worth arranging. Framed photographs, books on bookshelves, candlesticks, trays – there are different ways these can be used so that they make a positive contribution. The point of an arrangement is to create a pattern by arranging objects so that each surface – whether it is a mantelpiece, shelf or tabletop – makes its own picture. Objects dotted about the room lose their impact and relevance. The key is to experiment, relating objects by colour, texture and shape – a collection of patterned jugs on a shelf, an arrangement of blue glass on a tabletop.

Look at the overall shape of the arrangement. Displays that are regimented, rigidly symmetrical, or lined up in neat rows are deadening, but at the same time deliberately placing objects askew in a 'casual' fashion always looks contrived. An arrangement should be natural and full of movement.

A good arrangement also has a dynamic quality that arises from surprise and contrast. For example, the display of round, plain coloured period glass on the sewing table in the living room works only because of the juxtaposition of a patterned, angular, modern ceramic. Without the addition of this piece, the end result would look flat, just a group of similar objects.

COLLECTIONS

Favourite objects, pictures, flowers and books give a room meaning. The extra layer of colour, pattern and texture provided by an arrangement may be almost as important as its aesthetic contribution.

Each item in a collection tells its own story. It expresses your enjoyment of the thing itself, reminds you of the pleasure of discovery – the moment you bought it, the person who gave it to you – and acts as a constant source of impressions.

Collections can be changed easily and often to provide something fresh and new to look at. It is not necessary for every interesting or decorative object you own to be out on view – you can always put some things away until there is occasion to rediscover them. This may sound like an obvious point, but people sometimes decide against buying an object that intrigues them because there is no immediate use for it or place for it to go. In the same way, do not be intimidated by status or provenance. What counts is not the fact that a bowl is of rare porcelain and worth a fortune, but that it brings vitality to a room. If a piece has this quality it has value: junk shop finds are as valid as expensive antiques.

For original pieces that add a sense of personal feeling to a room, there is nothing better than handmade craftwork. In Britain, as in other countries, there is a great source of talent, flourishing in disciplines as diverse as weaving and ceramics. By supporting young craftspeople you can help to keep traditions alive; in exchange, you acquire for a reasonable price individual and beautiful pieces which have been made with

Above Fireplaces are natural focal points for arrangements.

care and enthusiasm. In many people's minds, the word 'craft' summons up an image of dreary brown pots, dull and worthy. Nothing could be further from the truth. The work of young designers, artists and craftspeople often expresses an interest in extending the scope of the medium, challenging and reinterpreting traditional methods of decoration.

My passion has always been for ceramics. I find the combination of the sculptural modelling of the clay and the painterly application of glazes constantly intriguing. The work of modern potters such as Janice Tchalenko and Carol McNichol continues to provide me with a rich source of inspiration and delight through their innovative designs.

HANGING PICTURES
Pictures on walls can be treated just like decorative objects arranged on a surface. The same principles apply. Small

paintings, drawings or photographs have more impact if they are hung as a group, fairly close together.

A group of pictures should have a certain affinity. The group in the living room began as a collection of black-and-white works on paper. After a while, I added a few coloured pictures as a contrast. In a collection all the frames do not have to be the same; on the contrary, if they are different this will help maintain and enhance the individuality of each picture. Unless I want a pair of pictures to align strictly with each

Above Pictures gain impact when hung together as a collection.

other, I do not take measurements before hanging. However, if you are hanging a collection it can be useful to lay out the pictures you want to display on the floor and experiment with different arrangements until the pattern emerges. It can also be a good idea to first prop up a picture – against the wall or on a tabletop, for example – and live with it for a while to get an idea of how it will look in that position.

ARRANGING FLOWERS

Flowers are at home in every room in the house; in the living room and hall, in particular, they provide a special welcome, a sense of refreshment and grace. The art of choosing and arranging flowers is similar to the art of creating any other type of display: it involves a sensitive response to colour, texture and shape; an eye for making patterns and an instinct for surprise and wit. It has nothing whatsoever to do with erecting rigid, complex constructions using foam blocks and wire, the type of awkwardly formal and unnatural display beloved of old-fashioned florists and flower-arranging schools.

A flower arrangement should be composed within the context of its setting. Flowers can literally flow out of the interior decoration. Coordinate arrangements with the existing colours of walls and soft furnishings; choose cottage flowers to perpetuate a nostalgic, country theme, elegant lilies to emphasize the clean lines of a contemporary interior. Flowers can also be highly effective as a contrast – a splash of brazen colour; humble posies adding a homely touch to formal or traditional rooms; exotic hothouse species providing a dramatic statement in a simple uncluttered setting.

Every parameter – colour, texture, shape – can suggest many ways of creating arrangements. There is nothing wrong with a display of flowers all of the same type and colour, or even a single beautiful bloom in a plain vase. If you extend the idea further, you can group different species of the same colour, or group a series of flowers of the same colour in different containers. In the same way, you can experiment by arranging flowers or foliage according to texture or line and shape to create a different effect.

With confidence, practice and a degree of intuition it is possible to create arrangements of great subtlety and flair, combining different species, colours and forms to make a unified, harmonious composition. But in every case an important consideration is the type of container and the style, colour, texture and form that it contributes to the display. For example, you might emphasize the fragility and delicate colour of sweet peas by placing them in a glass vase, allow country roses and honeysuckle to overflow a wicker basket, or assemble a collection of bright ceramic pots and jugs to underline a bold, vibrant display.

Above left A splash of colour on the hall table — delphiniums, camellias and hydrangeas, together with Matthew Hilton candlesticks and a Bruce McLean jug.

Above centre Scarlet and cerise nerines and fennel arranged in Judy Kaplan pots.

Above right Delphiniums and Royal Gold lilies are beautifully set off by camellia leaves, willow and fennel.

Below left Pale lilac roses, delphiniums and nerines in a Janice Tchalenko jug.

Below right Hydrangeas in a simple glass container; bowls by Emmanuel Cooper.

Far right A collection of Italian glass fruit.

LIGHTING FOR EFFECT

The living room is an area where lighting can be designed to enhance decoration, add drama and definition and adjust proportions. Lighting for effect – rather than for strictly functional purposes – is an important part of the interior.

When choosing lights for living rooms, most people tend to concentrate on the style of the fitting, neglecting to turn the light on to see how it works – how the light falls, the colour of the light source itself and how the light affects the way neighbouring colours are perceived. Naturally, the style of fitting is important, but it is the way in which the light is used which will have maximum impact.

In living rooms, as in other areas, two principal types of lighting are required: lighting which provides general or background illumination and lighting which accentuates specific areas. For general illumination, we use floor-standing or wall-mounted uplighters, which direct light, as the name suggests, up to the ceiling. If the ceiling is painted white, light will be reflected back down again, a particularly effective way of raising the overall light level without creating the harsh glare associated with overhead fittings. Uplighters also tend to increase the impression of space, dissolving angles in the corners of a room.

Accent lighting is provided by adjustable work lights which can be angled to direct the light down onto a surface. These pools of light add drama to a room, defining conversation areas and adding sparkle to points of interest.

Below and right All the light fittings in the house are plain black metal. These simple modern fittings have a certain sculptural beauty, which acts as a counterpoint to the vivid colours and rich patterns.

PIPING AND TRIM

The imaginative use of piping and trim can add contrast, humour and definition to a colour scheme. A piped edging, for example, acts rather like a picture frame, giving life to the object that it surrounds.

When preparing trim there is a temptation to use the same pattern as the main fabric or to pick out one of its predominant colours: this approach may work well, particularly if you do not want to emphasize an outline, but it should never be an automatic choice. A closely coordinated range of piping fabrics which are chosen to impose a unity over diverse patterns in a room may look predictable; however, the proportion of piping to main fabric is small, so by being adventurous in your choice of colours and patterns, you can create dramatic effects.

By experimenting with a colour board before selecting your piping you will discover a range of exciting and exotic contrasts. It is interesting and fun to use your selection of colours and patterns to link objects one to another; for example, you might select a colour used on a stool and reflect it in the piping used on a chair. In the living room, one of the ottomans that is covered in a sumptuous yellow satin fabric has been piped in black, to add strong graphic definition, while on the sofa some solid-coloured cushion covers are piped with a patterned fabric that occurs elsewhere in the room.

The opportunities for creating original colour contrasts between fabrics and objects are unlimited and the result of this approach is more natural as well as more lively than an over-coordinated scheme. Using piping and trim to add detail and definition in this way can really pay off, in the same way that buying exactly the right accessories for an outfit can create a delightful finishing touch. Only a slice of the fabric design will be visible in a piping or a trim, but if this is what is needed to bring an object to life then it can be well worth buying that extra length of fabric.

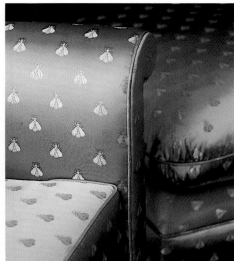

MAKING AND USING PIPING

Although piping is a small additional detail on items such as cushions and upholstered furniture, its impact can vary according to the fabric that is used. Piping of one colour used on a variety of different-patterned fabrics can have a unifying effect on a decorative scheme, while piping of a patterned fabric used against a plain colour can highlight the patterned fabric when it appears elsewhere in a room. The following instructions show how to prepare corded piping cut on a bias.

TECHNIQUE

To cut bias strips, bring one raw edge (cross grain) to lie along the selvedge and press. Unfold the fabric and use a ruler and pencil to draw lines parallel to the pressed foldline, marking out the strips. The strips must be wide enough to cover the piping cord and include two seam allowances.

Cut out the strips. Join them at right angles with right sides together and with 6mm (¼in) seam allowances, to make up the required length. Press seams open.

To make a long, continuous strip, take a piece of fabric at least twice as long as it is wide. Fold it diagonally as already described, and cut off the corner. With right sides facing and taking a 6mm (¼in) seam allowance, join this corner to the other edge. Mark strips parallel to the raw edges, then trim away the selvedges. Mark points A and B as shown, 6mm (¼in) in from the edges. With right sides together, pin A to B and continue pinning until you have a tube of fabric with a marked line running in a spiral from top to bottom. Stitch and press the seam, then cut along the marked line.

Fold the fabric strip over the piping cord, right side out and raw edges matching. Pin and stitch close to the cord, using a zipper foot.

Lay the prepared piping on the right side of one of the pieces to be seamed, matching the stitching line of the piping to the fabric seamline. Pin and stitch in

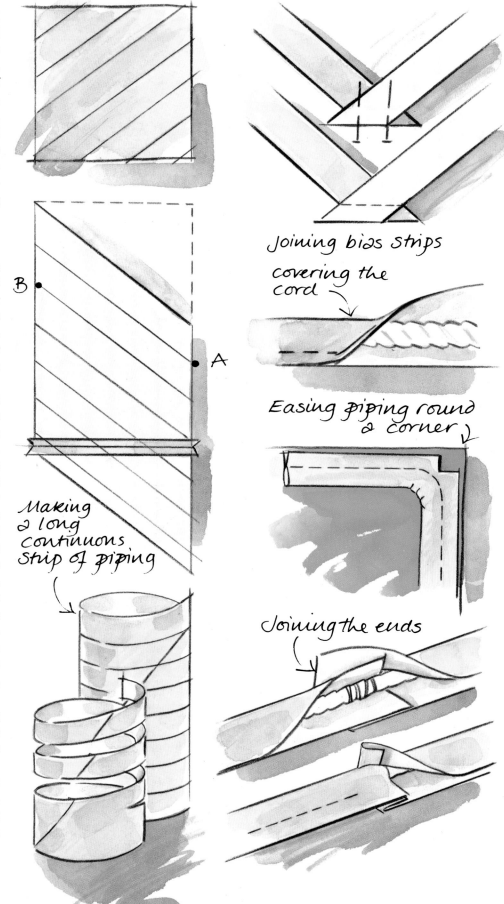

Joining bias strips

covering the cord

Easing piping round a corner

Making a long continuous strip of piping

Joining the ends

place with a zipper foot. Take corners at a slight curve, cutting the seam allowance of the piping up to the stitching line, as shown.

With right sides together, pin the second piece of fabric to the piped piece, matching raw edges. Pin and stitch through all layers, stitching close to the piping so that the previous lines of stitching are covered.

To join ends, unpick the casing at each end. If you are using fine cord or if there will be no strain on the piping, simply butt the cord ends against each other. For a firmer join, overlap the cord ends by about 2cm ($\frac{3}{4}$in), then unravel the ends and trim back one strand from one end and two from the other. Twist the remaining three strands together and secure them with thread. Join the fabric ends, either as described above for bias strips, or by turning one edge under and bringing it over the other raw edge and stitching. Try to position the join in line with a seam or – on a cushion, for example – centred between two corners.

PLAIN PIPED CUSHION

To make a plain piped cushion, cut a front and back to the same size. Prepare piping and stitch it around the seamline of the front piece. Join the front to back at one side only, stitching in from each corner and leaving an opening for the zip. Tack the opening temporarily then fold out the seam allowance of the back cover and press. Place the open zip face downwards (with teeth butting against piping). With front cover still folded away, pin, tack and stitch zip to front seam allowance. Open out cover and stitch the other side of zip to the back of the cover through all layers, taking the stitching across at the ends. Open the zip, remove tacks, then fold the cover so that right sides are together, and stitch up the remaining sides. Trim and turn.

Right The contrast piping of these solid-coloured cushions adds definition and a luxurious finish.

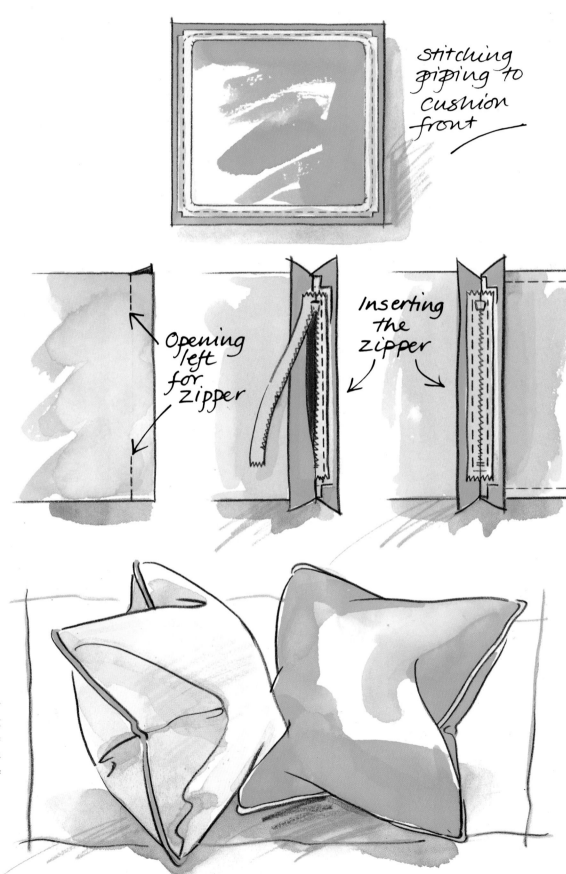

stitching piping to cushion front

Opening left for zipper

Inserting the zipper

PADDED FURNITURE

Many small items of furniture, such as stools, footstools or box seats, can be easily padded and covered with fabric, without the need of any advanced upholstery techniques. Not every piece of wood furniture is an antique that deserves to be noticed and, with a little ingenuity, many finds from second-hand shops can be transformed when covered with an interesting fabric.

The treatment is also worth considering if you want to soften the outline of a piece of furniture or blend it into the background by covering it with the same fabric used for other soft furnishings in the room. Alternatively, you may wish to use a covering in a contrasting design to add an accent of colour to a room.

TECHNIQUE

Providing you plan every stage of the job carefully in advance, an ability to work neatly is the main requirement. Obviously the simpler the design of the furniture, the easier it will be to cover. A straight-sided box seat with a separate cushion would be a good item to start with, but if you want to experiment with a stool then it is best to choose a style where the legs run down flush with the sides of the seat. If they are recessed under the seat, you will have more trouble cutting and fitting the pieces. Similarly, the more square-cut the design, the less trouble you will have in shaping the fabric.

In addition to the top fabric, you will need bump (the thick interlining generally used for curtains) and seating foam for the padding. You will also need a staple gun or upholstery tacks and a hammer, furniture glides for the feet, fabric glue, a fine, curved upholstery needle and upholstery pins. These last items are not essential but, being longer than ordinary dressmaking pins, they are easier to handle.

To cover an item of furniture, for example a stool, first take accurate measurements of all surfaces including the

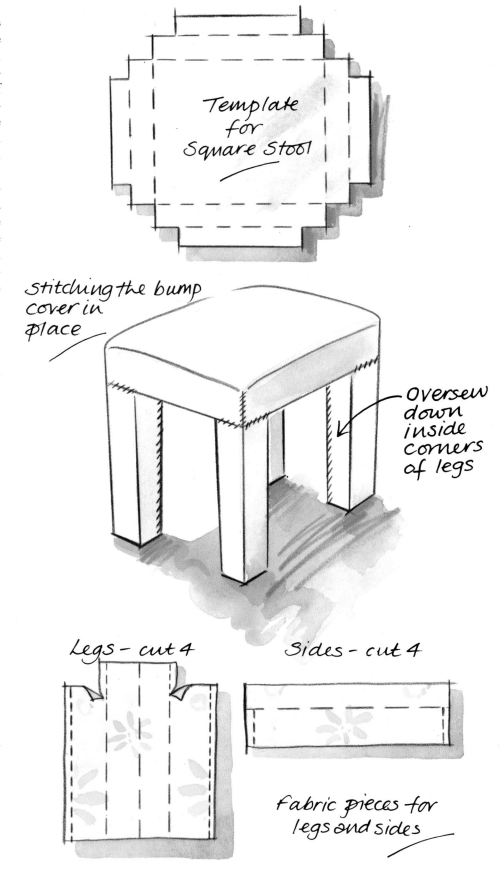

Template for Square Stool

stitching the bump cover in place

Oversew down inside corners of legs

Legs – cut 4

Sides – cut 4

fabric pieces for legs and sides

underside of the seat, and work out the best order of sewing, using a paper model or perhaps even cutting and pinning old sheeting. Make a paper template of the surface area of the top of the stool, then use it to mark and cut out foam that is 2.5cm (1in) thick. Lay the foam on the top of the stool and cover it with enough bump, to reach down the sides of the stool. Staple the bump to the underside of the frame, then neatly oversew the corner seams. Wrap a length of bump around each leg and oversew down the inside edge and to the sides of the seat cover as shown.

Adding 1.5 cm ($\frac{1}{2}$in) seam allowances all round, cut out the fabric for the cover: a top, four sides (deep enough to bring round to the underside of the seat), four legs (from top edge to floor, plus a turning at floor level), and an under-seat section. Stitch piping around the top piece; stitch side seams of leg and side pieces together as shown, cutting into the seam allowances at the corners, as necessary. Join to the piped top. Fit the cover over the stool, fold in raw edges on inside legs and slipstitch together neatly.

Staple the turnings to the underside of the frame. To cover all staples and raw edges on the underside of the seat, make a template and cut out fabric adding 1.5cm ($\frac{1}{2}$in) seam allowances as before. Fold in raw edges and glue in place.

To neaten the base of the legs, fold under the turnings and hammer on furniture glides to cover the raw edges.

Right Three different examples of padded stools which demonstrate the versatility of this upholstery technique.

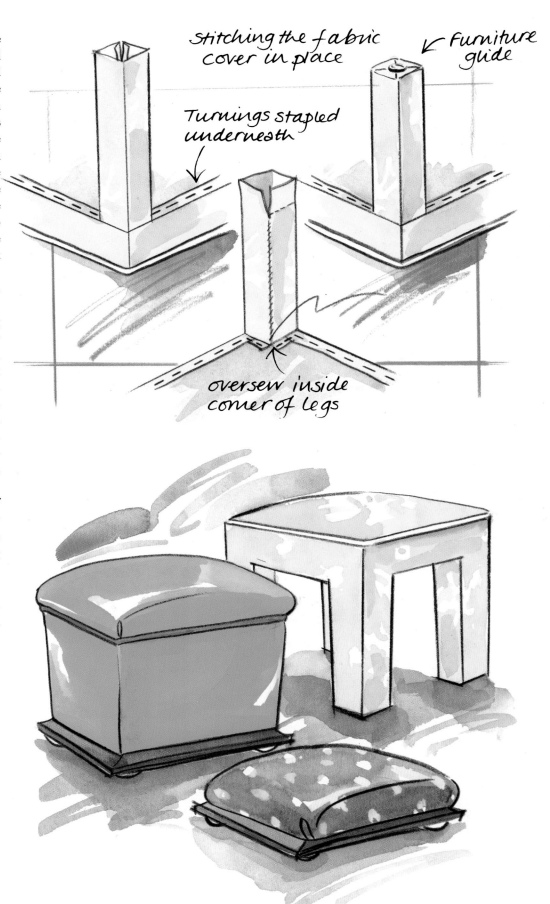

stitching the fabric cover in place

furniture glide

Turnings stapled underneath

oversew inside corner of legs

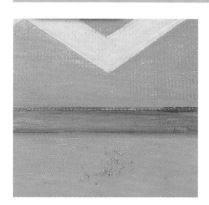

THE
MORNING
ROOM

If you work at home all or part of the time, it is important to have a space to call your own. Small box rooms or spare rooms can be ideal for the purpose. However, if there is no extra space, it may be worth building an extension.

A house may be extended at ground level if the garden is big enough, although in the city, options are often more restricted and planning regulations can be stringent. Converting attic space is one solution; an adjacent flat roof, at the side or back of the house, is another natural site.

The morning room is the only completely new room in the house. Incorporating what was a small bathroom off the first-floor landing, it extends directly over the ground-floor study.

An extension can sometimes present a problem if its position blocks light from existing rooms. In this case, toplighting the new area with a large skylight had an immediate and beneficial impact. Even though it is essentially a private space for thinking, reading and working, I enjoy the sense of being connected with the rest of the house.

::

ARCHITECTURAL DETAIL

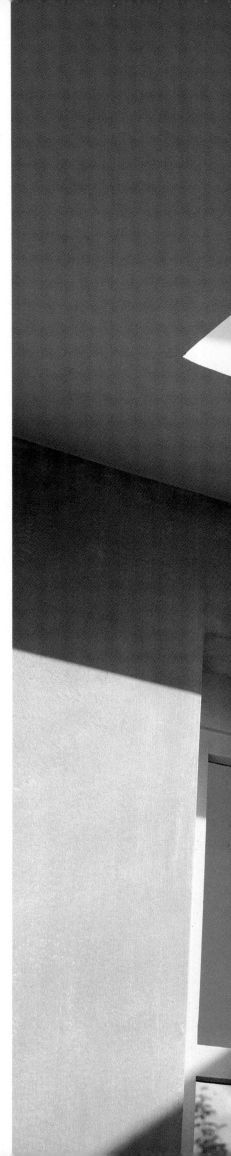

Building an entirely new room offers the opportunity to create new architectural detailing that is not merely applied but forms part of the actual structure of the space. The design of my morning room is based on the theme of a square. Elsewhere in the house, the square appears as a decorative motif on architraves, cupboard doors and so on, but in this room it is also used as a type of grid, determining the proportion, shape and size of various openings.

I particularly wanted a room that was as open and light as possible, with clear views of trees and sky – a true garden room. For this reason I decided to leave the room directly accessible, with no wall to divide it from the landing. Using the square as the basis of the design enabled us to incorporate different types and sizes of openings without destroying the unity of the space. The base of the skylight is a square. The windows and French doors are rectangles composed of square panels. The narrow strip window to the left of the desk is the width of a square pane: here, what had been a small bathroom window was simply extended down to the floor.

Because of this square grid, the extension is internally consistent. But any new building or extension is also viewed from the outside. I did not want the morning room to stand out as an obvious addition and so, to blend the new architectural style in with the original elevation, the windows and doors at the back of the house, beneath the level of the morning room, were changed so that they conformed to the square grid.

Above and right The morning room, with its skylight and large windows, has a strong sense of connection with the garden below. The design of all the windows is based on a square grid.

COLOURS AND TEXTURES

To promote an atmosphere of calm, the decoration is deliberately simple and uncluttered. Because I did not want the room to look like a direct extension of the landing, the walls are painted pink rather than the blue of the hall, although the blue is wrapped around the corner of one wall to tie the two spaces together.

To complement the clear, light colours of the walls and floor, the armchairs and cushions are covered in plain contrasting fabrics. Altogether, the large blocks of pink, green, white, yellow and blue-green give a 'cool' atmosphere, distinct from the richness and intensity of the shades used in the living room.

Above and right The morning room is decorated in clear, light colours with little pattern in evidence. This restraint is deliberate, so as to focus attention on the view. The patterns that do exist on rugs and blankets are geometric to emphasize the graphic quality of the architectural detailing. All the rag rugs were woven specially from fabrics used in the house.

DECORATIVE APPROACH

I use the morning room most often in the summer or whenever the light is good. Here I read, work, write letters and keep collections of magazines and postcards: the room has a contemplative feeling and is not intended to accommodate many people. With its large windows and skylight creating an impression of sitting in the middle of the garden, this room is also the place where I keep gardening books and tend to plan the garden.

The structure and contemporary detailing of the morning room mean that it is not nostalgic. Although I once considered having an old desk, I rejected the idea in favour of a modern glass-and-metal table which better suits the character and scale of the room. Similarly, I did not want to fill the space with plants, which would inevitably have evoked a conservatory atmosphere. Instead, there are cut flowers arranged in plain-coloured ceramic containers and a few exotic growing plants such as an amaryllis and palms. Because the real pictures are what you can see out of the windows, there are only a few pictures hanging on the wall; those that are there are in subtle black and white.

Beneath the shelves holding gardening books and personal things are panels covering the radiators. These are pierced top and bottom with rows of square cutouts, and painted on the floor directly in front of them are identical white squares – as if light shining through the grilles made a pattern on the floor.

All the new architectural detailing – doors, window frames and skirting boards – are white. Because the rest of the woodwork is plain and there is no decorative plasterwork, the new skirting boards, with their pattern of three incised parallel lines, are an important element. And, since the room opens directly off the landing, the new skirting boards meet the grey of the original skirtings in the hall and stairway – not an integration, but a direct, forthright conjunction of old and new.

As a floor covering to link the two spaces, coir matting would have been an option, with the aim of integrating the space with the hall, but instead a hard floor was chosen. This new pine surface is painted in a pattern of green and white checks, pursuing the fresh, summery theme (see pages 66–67). To design a painted floor, either treat the pattern as if it were a carpet, running uniformly wall to wall, or as a rug, which need not necessarily be centred. For this area, I felt that a 'rug' design would be more appropriate and have more vitality than one that was centred and symmetrical.

The floor design of the morning room was carefully developed to echo the architectural details of the room and to give a variation on the square motif that is found throughout the house. Painting a floor in this way entails a fair amount of work, so it makes sense to put considerable effort into the design, ensuring that it will suit the architecture of the room as well as the major items of furniture.

Do you want an off-centre rug-type design, as in the morning room, or would a wall-to-wall pattern be preferable? Would the shape and architecture of the room be best complemented by a medallion-type floor design, radiating out from a central point? Or would an understated, all-over finish provide the right background to your furniture?

The first stage in working out a design is to measure the room accurately and draw the outline to scale on squared paper. Make several copies so that you can experiment with different possibilities. Once a design is chosen, make a series of colour experiments on paper.

Above far left Anemones and geranium leaves in 1940s Fiestaware containers.

Below far left Books and a letter rack covered in marbled paper.

Above left A narrow glass table provides room for a display of flowers.

Below left Disparate objects, including a ceramic dish by Liz Hodges.

THE PAINTED FLOOR

In the morning room the floorboards were new. If your floorboards are old, they should be prepared before painting: secure loose boards and hammer in any protruding nails using a nail punch. Cracks or large holes can be filled with wedges of wood of a similar type to that used for the original boards; cut them to size and hammer them home to lie just below the surface of the floor. The floor can then be sanded with an industrial sander, which can be easily hired.

When the floor is smooth and clean, you can transfer the design.

MARKING OUT A DESIGN

To mark a square design on a floor use pencil or chalk. It is best to find the centre of the room and use this as a point of reference, working outwards. First find the centre of two opposite walls and, using two nails to mark these points, tie a length of heavily chalked string between them. Snap the taut string against the floor to mark the centre. The mid-point of the line is the centre of the room. Using your diagram for reference, mark the two outer edges of the design that are at right angles to the marked centre line.

The important point to remember is that the ratio between the distances should always be 3:4:5, as shown in the diagram opposite.

Mark points where the edges of each square will fall on the outer edges of the design, then join the marked points to make lines parallel to the centre line. Mark the intersections on the centre line, and an outer line parallel to it, then join these points to complete the squares.

THE PAINT TECHNIQUE

The paint technique used for the morning-room floor was very similar to that already described for the walls in the hall (see page 32), but in this case oil-based paints were used for greater durability.

Painting within the lines of a design is not easy, although slight inaccuracies can sometimes add to the charm. One way to work is to screen off areas with masking tape, but this can damage the paintwork, so it is often better to score the wood very lightly by running a utility knife along the design lines. The slight indentation will then help to prevent paint from running over the lines.

The first coat of paint used on the morning room floor was thinned with white spirit so that it would soak into the wood and seal it without obscuring the grain. Cadmium and viridian green paint were mixed into white for the green squares, and white was softened with raw umber and black to make an off-white for the white squares. Care was taken to keep the colours within the pencilled lines.

Three more coats of paint in varying, purer tones of green and white were lightly dragged in the direction of the grain. In each case some of the layers were allowed to show through, as if the floor had been painted several times, using similar colours on each occasion. Finally, pure white was dragged over the white squares to highlight them, while the green squares were lightly dragged in an off-white, using paint straight from the can in uneven strokes in order to form an irregular finish of varying colour tones.

Painted floors are generally sealed with varnish, but this finish can have a yellowing effect and make a floor look *too* protected. In this case a water-based acrylic varnish was used to seal the floor. It is not quite as tough as polyurethane but has a far less yellowing effect, and in any case the floor in the morning room is not subjected to heavy use.

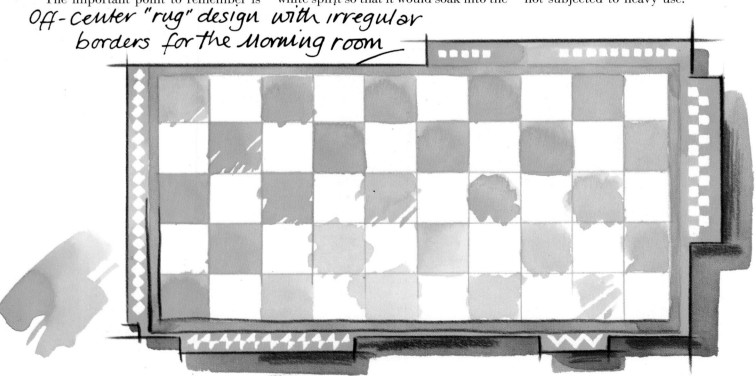

Off-center "rug" design with irregular borders for the Morning room

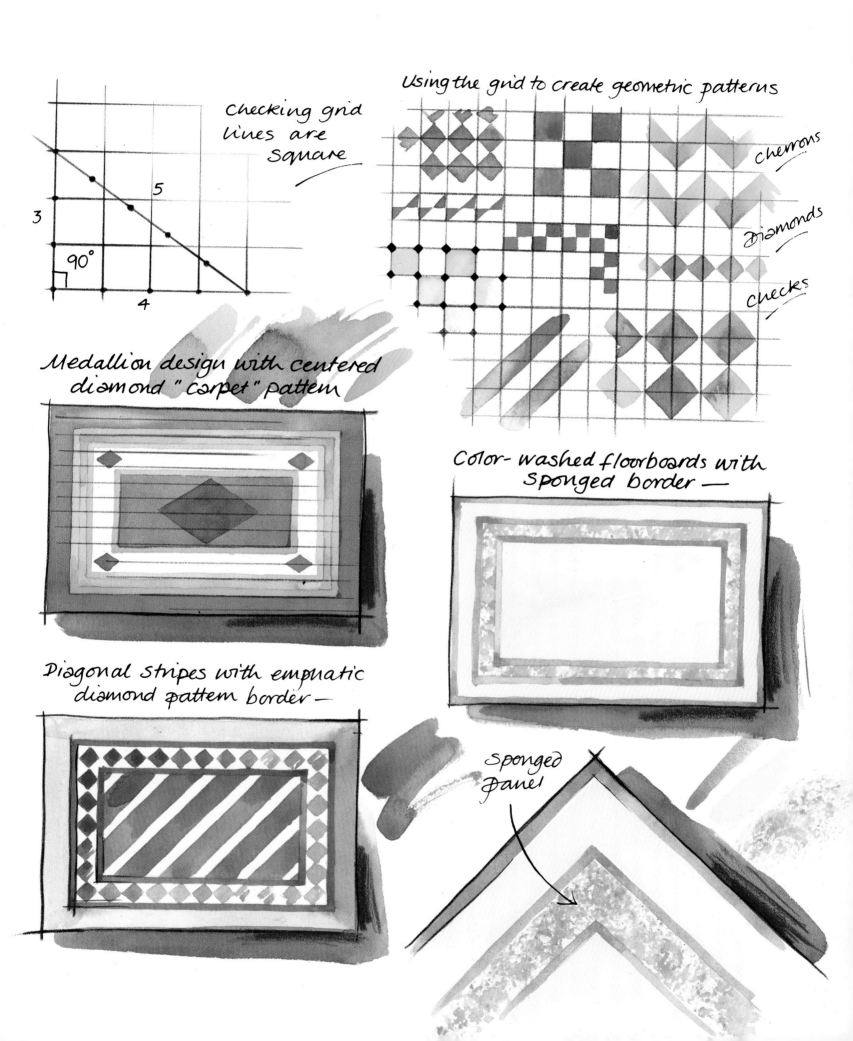

checking grid lines are square

5

3

90°

4

Using the grid to create geometric patterns

chevrons

diamonds

checks

Medallion design with centered diamond "carpet" pattern

Color-washed floorboards with sponged border —

Diagonal stripes with emphatic diamond pattern border —

Sponged panel

THE STUDY

For the designer, it is always a challenge not only to use space in the best possible way but also to respond to different tastes and needs and to give each room its own distinct feeling and atmosphere. The study is directly beneath the morning room. Although the two rooms are identical in floor area and both overlook the garden, they are vastly different from each other in style as well as character.

The design of a small room can be approached in different ways. You can keep colours light and bright, restrict pattern and clutter to a minimum and, as in the case of the morning room, create a sense of space and expansion with large windows and rooflights so that the room 'breathes'. In this room we decided to ignore the fact that space was limited and fill the room with intense colour, rich patterns, and pictures.

This study was originally a cloakroom, which contained a fireplace and had a small bathroom and a boxroom leading off to either side of the entrance. During the conversion of the house it was decided to remove the bathroom and, rather than waste space by retaining an extravagant cloakroom, turn the area into a study.

::

DECORATION AND DETAIL

The initial thoughts about the decoration of this room were that it should have fabric-covered walls to create an intimate atmosphere. Instead, however, the walls were painted a strong bright yellow. This works, not least because the intense colour provides a sparkling view when glimpsed from the end of the hall.

Throughout the room there is a theme of contrasting flower and geometric patterns. The sofa is covered with a print called *Fiorita* ('little flowers'), a design of lilacs and stripes, here used in a terracotta, burgundy and blue colourway. The same red and blue appear in the upholstery of the stool, which is covered in *Striato*, a geometric design. Cushions piled on the sofa add a mosaic of pattern, including *Giardino*, a large floral print, and *Acanthus*, both from the *Grandiflora* collection.

Black is used positively as a tool to cut through the richness of the decoration and underline the graphic quality of the new architectural details. Black edging on the blinds echoes the black of the picture frames. The leather chair and modern desk lamp also provide relief from the patterned surfaces.

Other plain colours work to set up relationships and rhythms, pulling the different elements together. The same green of the blind appears on a cushion cover and on piping. Blue, echoing the colour of the hall walls, is displayed by the blanket, rag rug and painted table.

In addition there are ceramics; a mass of pictures, and objects; these form patterns of their own and create the strong sense of personality which is the room's particular attraction.

Left The sofa, upholstered in *Fiorita*, is piled with cushions of contrasting colours.

Above right Books covered in a mixture of marbled papers.

Below right A blanket woven by Richard Womersley adds a touch of blue.

Below far right A bright green Roman blind crisply edged in black.

MAKING SPACE WORK

There is no reason why a small room should not be bright and busy; the advantage of this approach is that a cosy intimate atmosphere is immediately created and the space paradoxically seems bigger because so much is going on within it.

Here the original fireplace was removed. In such a small area a fireplace could never be used without scorching anyone sitting in front of it; even unlit, it would have had a claustrophobic and dominating effect on the room. By excavating the chimney breast above to the width and depth of the fireplace, it was possible to create a natural space for storage without losing any floor area. The portions of wall left at either side now serve as pillars supporting shelves in the centre and at the sides – a convenient place for books, photographs, hi-fi equipment and favourite objects.

Above A shelf devoted to an arrangement of brightly coloured and richly patterned vases and jugs makes a glowing centrepiece.

Right and far right The wide-base shelf holds a collection of larger containers as well as providing storage space for hi-fi equipment and television.

SHELVING

In any house there will be a certain amount of potential clutter – books, magazines, records, cassettes, discs, files, photographs and other mementoes. My own preference for storing such objects is shelving, since fitted cupboards can be inconvenient to use and tend to impose restrictions on the arrangement and decorative rhythm of a room. Provided objects are carefully arranged on shelves, they can look interesting and attractive, and it is convenient to have everything you need to hand.

Shelving can sometimes look obtrusive, but this need not be the case. Well-planned shelves can complement and reinforce the architecture and décor of a room. In my house there are deep, chunky shelves in the living room, the morning room, the study and the kitchen. These are painted to match the walls and are constructed with invisible brackets so that they appear to be part of the walls, rather than being tacked on as an afterthought.

In the study, the morning room and the kitchen, the shelves are fitted into existing alcoves, while those in the living room run along one wall. At one end, the wall acts as a natural stop, at the other there is a support butted up against the side of the door frame. The top shelf extends over the lintel of the door so that the shelving creates a frame around the door and forms part of the architectural detailing of the room. All these shelves are made of medium-density fibreboard, a very strong material which, when decorated, resembles a plastered surface.

The concealed brackets that hold the shelves in place are attached to substantial metal supports that are built into the walls and are essential for shelves over 1m (1yd) long. It is preferable to get a skilled carpenter to construct shelves of this type since it is a complicated process that is best carried out by an experienced professional.

Shorter shelves that are designed to fit into a small alcove can be supported by

1
Wall of shelving "tailored" for intended use

2
Shelving framing doorway – creates "entrance"

wooden battens, concealed within a frame. If, as often happens, the alcove is wider at the back than the front, the shelving cannot be slipped over the battens. In this case the bottom section must be screwed in place from underneath. Provided the screws are countersunk, they will not be visible when the holes have been plugged and the shelf painted.

Because this type of shelving is not adjustable, it is essential to plan ahead as far as possible. Consider the different types of objects that each shelf will hold. Will you, for example, need some extra deep shelves at a low level to carry hi-fi equipment? Should some shelves be set closer together than others, to avoid wasting space, and can this be done without destroying the sense of architectural unity? If the shelving is planned as an integral part of the room, then it will become a decorative feature, not just a practical necessity.

Shelving can be designed to make use of unusual angles or space which would otherwise be 'dead'. Wherever possible, the design should complement existing architectural detailing.

1. A system of shelves covering an entire wall should be planned with reference to what will eventually be stored there. A wide-base shelf takes heavier and larger items while a narrow shelf provides space for storing small, awkward-shaped objects.

2. If a wall contains a doorway, shelving can be extended round the opening like a frame — a design which integrates with the existing structure and detail, adding interest and conserving space.

3. Shelves built-in under a sloping ceiling exploit rather than disguise the planes and angles of the space which could otherwise look awkward.

4. An alternative for a room with a sloping ceiling is to build the shelves at the lowest point — where there is insufficient headroom and space would otherwise be wasted making the room seem smaller than it really is.

3
Shelving built-in under a sloping ceiling

4
Shelves under low ceiling — where floor unusable

ROMAN BLINDS

The Roman blinds described here are Tricia Guild's variation on the standard Roman blind (or shade) as it exists in America. Tricia's construction is slightly different – with carriers running horizontally across the width of the blind, a lath strip inside the bottom carrier, and a dowel in each of the remaining carriers.

The fabric folds are formed by a system of cords running vertically through rings attached to the back of the blind. The entire blind is attached to a mounting board at the top, and screwed to the wall or window frame. The blinds here have rings attached to horizontal carriers through which lengths of dowel are inserted, to prevent sagging.

The blinds are simple to make, provided you follow the instructions carefully. Any deviation from the placement lines for the carriers will make the finished blind hang crookedly. Choose a good quality cotton and make sure that the lining fabric is of a similar quality.

Cut the main fabric to the desired finished size of the blind, adding $2\frac{1}{4}$in

(6cm) to the width and $4\frac{1}{2}$in (12cm) to the length. Cut the lining to the same length and to the finished blind width less $\frac{3}{4}$in (2cm) to allow for $\frac{3}{4}$in (2cm) of main fabric to show on the right side. Allow extra lining fabric for the carriers.

Additionally, you will need a staple gun; a 2in × 1in (5cm × 2.5cm) mounting board cut to the finished width of the blind; fixing screws to install mounting board; lengths of $\frac{1}{2}$in (1.2cm) dowel, one for each carrier, $\frac{3}{4}$in (2cm) shorter than the width of the blind, and one strip of 1in (2.5cm) lath, the same length, for the bottom edge of the blind. Every carrier has a ring at each end so that the blind can be drawn up in neat folds. For the two vertical rows that the rings form, you will need an eye screw and cord twice the length of the blind plus the width.

With wrong sides together, join the main fabric and lining down each long side with a $\frac{3}{8}$in (1cm) seam. Press seams open, then turn through to the right side and press the side edges, with an even $\frac{3}{4}$in (2cm) of main fabric showing down each side edge on the back of the blind. Treating the double fabric as one, turn up first $\frac{3}{4}$in (2cm), then $1\frac{1}{2}$in (4cm) along the bottom edge. Press and stitch close to the folded edge, leaving the sides open so that the lath can be inserted later.

Lay the blind wrong side up on a flat surface, pinning the layers together at the top and smoothing out any wrinkles. Using a pencil and long ruler, draw a horizontal line across the top of the blind, $2\frac{1}{4}$in (6cm) down from the top raw edge. Use a set square to check that this line is at right angles to the sides. Adjusting the spacing to fit the length, draw placement lines for the carriers, about 10in to 12in (25cm to 30cm) – twice the depth of the finished folds – apart. The lowest line should be a half fold up from the machine stitching of the hem.

To make the carriers, cut strips of lining fabric $3\frac{1}{4}$in (8cm) wide and of a length that is the width of the blind plus $\frac{1}{2}$in (1.5cm). For each one, turn in and

press a $\frac{3}{8}$in (1cm) allowance along each long edge; bring the pressed edges together and press a center crease. Holding the strip open, very carefully pin the center crease to the marked placement line (with pressed edges facing), leaving the ends of the carrier strips extending.

With thread to match the front, machine along the pinned center crease line of the carrier, removing pins as you work and stopping $\frac{1}{8}$in (3mm) short of the side edges of the blind. Turn in the short ends of the carrier, then bring the folded long edges together and stitch close to the edge, leaving the ends open at either side.

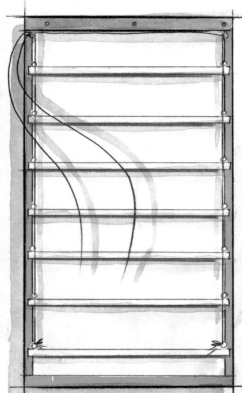

Knot the cords together at the top, just outside the edge of the blind.

Holding the fabric clear, screw the mounting board in place. Attach the cleat to the side of the windows.

To make the same type of blind with a finished edging ¾in (2cm) wide, cut edging strips 2¼in (6cm) wide and cut the main fabric and lining ¾in (2cm) less than the finished total width of the blind. Turn in ⅜in (1cm) along the long sides of the edging strip and press. Match the "right" side of the edging strip to the side of the front of the blind. Sew the two edges together. Then, turn the edging strip out and around to the back side of the blind and join the free edge of the edging to the side edge of the back of the blind (forming a "tube"). Sew the edges together and press the tube flat. If you are also putting an edging strip along the bottom, position the lowest carrier so that the bottom edge of the blind will be visible below the pleats.

Prepare the mounting board for fixing in place by drilling and countersinking holes for the screws at regular intervals. The short side edges will be visible, so paint them to match the window frame or glue spare fabric over them. Lay the blind flat, wrong side up. Turn the top edge inside for ¾in (2cm) to neaten, then lay the mounting board on the blind, carefully matching the top front edge of the board to the top placement line. Bring the fabric over the board and staple it at 3in (7.5cm) intervals. Fix eye screws to the underside of the board, one in line with each vertical line of rings.

Insert the dowels into the carriers and the bottom lath into the hem pocket. Close the side ends of the carriers with a few stitches. At the pulling side of the blind, tie cord to the bottom ring, thread the cord up through the rings above and then through the eye screw at the top. Repeat for the other row(s), always finishing by taking the cord across the top of the blind and through the eye screw on the pulling side of the blind.

THE KITCHEN AND DINING ROOM

In our house, all of us are avid cooks. My husband, who is a restaurateur, has a professional interest in the ergonomics of kitchen design. Consequently, the kitchen was planned to suit two people working. Because we also enjoy entertaining, a large space for cooking and eating was called for, acknowledging the fact that people tend to congregate in kitchens; the bustle of behind-the-scenes activity, the aroma of food cooking and the anticipation of a convivial meal are always irresistible attractions for family and friends.

At the same time, without detracting from the warm and welcoming atmosphere, I wanted to make some kind of visual distinction between the cooking and eating areas. An entirely open-plan arrangement would have run the two activities together: the cook would have been left perpetually 'on stage' and eating would have become less of a celebratory event. Therefore there is a half-height barrier dividing the room, accommodating storage on the kitchen side and acting as a bar for guests on the other.

PLANNING A KITCHEN LAYOUT

Kitchen layout has been the subject of much theorizing and research. There are studies which seek to demonstrate optimum working heights and determine the ideal distances between centres of activity, and which recommend positions for services and appliances – all with the aim of making the 'work sequence' efficient for the kitchen user. If this sounds involved and rather scientific, do not worry: in practice, the basis of kitchen layout is really just common sense.

A kitchen must accommodate distinct areas where food is prepared, cooked and refrigerated, as well as provide storage for utensils, pots and pans and tableware. The relationship

between the three main focal points – the 'wet' area (sink), the 'cold' area (refrigerator) and the 'hot' area (oven and hob) – should be planned so that the process of cooking and preparing food is easy and safe. Once the basic layout has been determined you can go on to the next stage and plan the position of sockets and light fittings.

Ideally, one works in sequence around the layout, to avoid the awkwardness of having to retrace any steps. For safety reasons, electricity should be kept well away from water and, for the sake of efficiency, the refrigerator should not be too close to a heat source. Oddly enough, it is sometimes easier to

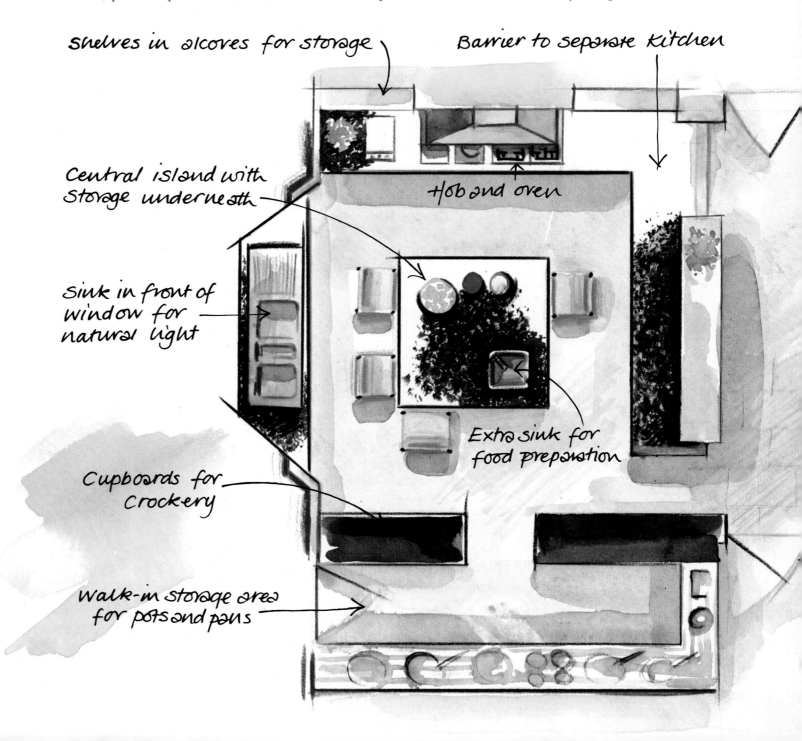

Shelves in alcoves for storage

Barrier to separate kitchen

Central island with storage underneath

Hob and oven

Sink in front of window for natural light

Extra sink for food preparation

Cupboards for crockery

Walk-in storage area for pots and pans

organize a small space more effectively than a large one: if the kitchen is too big, there may be too much movement from area to area to work efficiently.

With a big open space at our disposal, we could plan the kitchen from scratch. The size of the kitchen area was determined by the position of the barrier and the decision to build a storage wall, creating a walk-in cupboard to house crockery, pots and pans. The work area that remained was then planned around a square, with a square island in the centre.

The main sink is positioned in front of the window to benefit from natural light and to simplify drainage. On the adjacent side are the hob and oven, close to the preparation area; while on the opposite wall is the refrigerator, positioned quite close to the door so that food can be unloaded easily and people can serve themselves with drinks or snacks without having to walk right through the kitchen.

If there is enough space, central islands can be very useful and versatile, providing additional worktops as well as extra storage capacity. The island in our kitchen is plumbed with a small sink and most of the food preparation takes place here, but it is also big enough to serve as a table for eating informal meals when we are not entertaining.

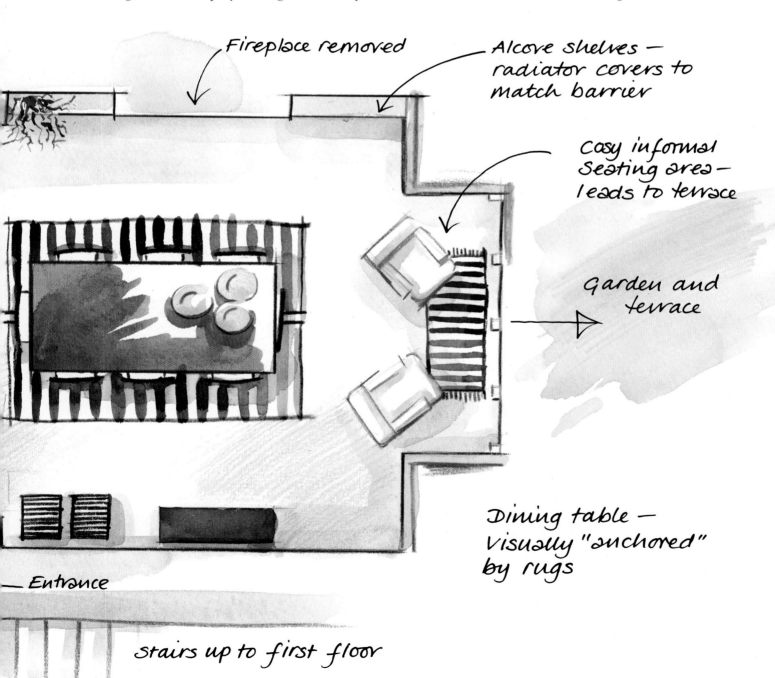

Fireplace removed

Alcove shelves — radiator covers to match barrier

Cosy informal seating area — leads to terrace

Garden and terrace

Dining table — visually "anchored" by rugs

Entrance

stairs up to first floor

SURFACES, TEXTURES AND DETAILS

Because the kitchen and dining areas were created from what had been a series of small basement rooms, the conversion work was necessarily so extensive that none of the original surfaces or details were left. This meant that the entire level could be treated in a contemporary way, with new architectural detailing.

The decorative scheme, as it evolved, concentrated more on changes of texture than on colour or pattern, again making a contrast with the rest of the house. The discovery of the original stone steps leading down to the basement led us to use stone for the kitchen/dining room floor – the same mellow French stone in large rectangular slabs that extends through the entrance hall (see page 29).

Building on this warm, neutral background, a variety of other naturally textured materials was chosen for other surfaces and finishes. The worktops throughout the kitchen area and on the island unit are made of rich, deep terracotta and black granite, this material being chosen in preference to marble or stone because it does not stain or mark. The cupboard doors are black, spattered with a fine spray of whites and greys – a low-key texture that does not compete with the granite tops.

All the kitchen units were chosen from a standard range, but the doors were removed and redesigned. The top of the barrier and the alcove shelves in the dining room are made of a paler version of the same stone used on the floor. And, while all these surfaces are essentially 'hard', their natural colours and textural depth mean that they appear soft, together creating a sense of enveloping warmth, a welcoming atmosphere for a room that is at the centre of family life.

New architectural detailing, using the square motif, unifies the different textures, appearing on door architraves, inset as cupboard handles and as a decorative detail on the stonework. But the alcoves in the kitchen and dining area have been kept as rounded arches – a slight touch of the past in a thoroughly modern room. For the same reason, the simple dining-room table, made of fruitwood, is not a contemporary piece.

Set against the natural materials and providing a graphic hard edge is the use of metal: black for light fittings, plugs and switches; chrome, aluminium and stainless steel for shelves, sinks, hob and hood, and the fine blinds at the kitchen window, as well as for the utensils and equipment that are displayed.

Above left and right The square motif inset in a stone shelf support and as cupboard handles.

Right Speckled quails' eggs on the granite worktop.

THE PLASTER AND FRESCO EFFECT

To harmonize with the flooring and increase the sense of light at this lower level, the walls needed to be warm, yet fairly neutral. What we set out to achieve was the appearance of raw, unpainted plaster. Because unfinished plaster continually forms a dusty layer, it should always be sealed; this process, however, turns the plaster mauve-pink and patchy, so the sealed plaster of the wall was treated simply as a base to which various natural, neutral tints were applied to restore the original look. The tints were rubbed in at random, and the result has great depth and texture without looking like a contrived paint finish.

Narrow lines were painted at the top and bottom of the walls to prevent them running together visually with the floor and ceiling. At the top, the lines are in terracotta and cream and are positioned roughly 2.5cm (1in) down from the ceiling. At the base of the wall, the lines are in deep terracotta and black; these were subsequently distressed to give them an aged look. The base line also serves to conceal the inevitable scuffs as well as the dark edge that tends to occur when floors are cleaned. The lines are unobtrusive, but they are just enough to give a crisp edge and a sense of detail.

Once the walls were finished, it was decided that a fresco effect would further enhance their aged quality. At the garden end of the dining area, a pattern of lemons and foliage was applied to the surface; a faded, elegant fresco, reminiscent of the Italian villas which have inspired me so much. Elsewhere, on the door surround at the entrance to the kitchen, a border, consisting of a broken architrave, was painted on. This has the quality of an architectural detail and adds a little humour to the room.

Left An arrangement of winter branches and beaten metal candlesticks in the dining room alcove sets off the plaster effect on the walls.

Above Examples of the 'fresco' decoration — surrounding the doorway as a painted architrave and on the wall beside the French windows.

STORAGE AND DISPLAY

Top Suspended from a metal rack are colanders, sieves, and graters.

Above left A collection of condiments in the kitchen alcove.

Above right Containers for preserved fruits, pickles and jams.

Right The storage area adjoining the kitchen, filled with metal shelving for pans, casseroles and cooking tins.

Kitchen storage must be supremely practical. Utensils and equipment that are frequently used should be accessible but should not clutter up worktops and preparation areas. And while some items can be put away in cupboards and drawers, many can remain on view, arranged on shelves or racks to contribute colour and interest.

Where you store or keep things should relate to the way you work. In our kitchen, the plates and dishes that are used most of the time are stored near the dishwasher; utensils are suspended from hanging racks over the island and hob; cutlery is kept in a drawer in the central island. Floor-to-ceiling shelves in the open walk-in cupboards are piled with ceramics, large dishes, casseroles, pots and pans. Although the shelves are away from the main area they are still on view. Below the worktops are flat-fronted cupboards, drawers and shelves for storing appliances, cleaning materials and other kitchen necessities. These give a functional, clean line that counteracts the busy look of the open alcove.

Except where it is absolutely necessary, I prefer not to store things out of sight. The kitchen is one area where even quite mundane household objects can make attractive arrangements. Colanders, sieves, whisks and graters appear almost sculptural when hanging from hooks and are also readily accessible at all times; brightly coloured jugs and plates, glasses, teapots and coffee pots always look good on open shelves. We often bring back special vinegars or cooking oils from our travels abroad; in their simple glass and earthenware containers, these make an intriguing collection. Other foodstuffs can be decanted into storage jars and kept on hand. I like the liveliness of a mixture of different types of jars and bottles as well as the interesting colour combinations of their contents, such as jams and preserves. It is not necessary to adopt one system of storage and adhere to it religiously.

LIGHTING IN WORK AREAS

Above Recessed halogen lamps in the ceiling create a sparkling pool of white light that filters through the kitchen utensils which are suspended over the central island.

Right The overhead lighting provides extra emphasis for the work area.

In a purely practical sense, the purpose of lighting is to provide even illumination, so that everyday activities can be performed safely and efficiently when natural light levels are low. Lighting can also be used as an additional accent, either to spotlight work areas or to accentuate decorative arrangements, paintings or architectural detail. But, most importantly, lighting can be a positive way of generating atmosphere and mood, and it is this decorative, intangible aspect that is often least understood.

Good lighting can transform the ambiance of a room; a sense of atmosphere arises when there are dramatic, overlapping pools of light, contrasts that lead the eye from area to area in a room. There is no better way to undo the best decorative efforts than by lighting a room uniformly from a single, central, bright overhead fitting.

As in the rest of the house, the lights in the kitchen and dining room are modern black metal fittings; here, they are either recessed ceiling downlights, fixed wall uplighters or accent spotlights. In the kitchen, directional recessed downlights are positioned over key work areas – around the perimeter worktop, over the island unit and under the stove hood. Pendant spotlights over the barrier create sparkling pools of light, accenting displays of flowers and fruit. Lighting in the dining area is provided by ceiling-mounted spotlights and wall-mounted uplighters on curved metal brackets.

Just as important as the type and position of the light fitting is the quality of the light source. The common domestic light source is the tungsten bulb. We have become accustomed to this type of light, but it does have a significantly yellow cast that alters colours and colour relationships, just as most fluorescent tubes produce an ugly green glare. Halogen lighting, a relatively new development, is by contrast a much truer light, closer in colour value to natural sunlight. It is a white light, sparkling and vital. Much used in today's shops and restaurants, it is now becoming more available for home interiors. We use halogen light throughout the house, but it is particularly beneficial in the kitchen because an important part of the presentation and enjoyment of food is an appreciation of its colours.

Lighting requirements often conflict, and this is particularly evident in open-plan/multi-purpose rooms such as a combined kitchen and dining area. On the one hand, specific work areas of the kitchen must be well lit, with both background and accent lighting; on the other, dining areas need softer, more evocative lighting.

One way of reconciling different lighting needs is to use dimmer switches to vary the levels of light. In this way, for example, kitchen lights which need to be reasonably bright for food preparation, can be lowered to provide just a background glow when the dining room is being used for entertaining.

THE DINING AREA

A separate dining room, devoted entirely to formal or evening meals, can make the experience of eating and entertaining very dramatic and special, a true celebration. But few houses or apartments today possess enough space to allocate a whole room to this activity, and dining areas now tend to be integrated into kitchens or living rooms.

In our dining area the fireplace was removed but the alcoves at either side of what used to be the chimney breast remain. Here, floor-to-ceiling shelves would have looked too cluttered, so instead of shelves a radiator was placed in each alcove, concealed behind decorative panels and topped with stone, creating an effect reminiscent of console tables.

One particular problem associated with a combined kitchen and dining room, aside from the lighting and layout difficulties already discussed, is that dining areas can look rather austere and empty when not being used, something that will be all the more noticeable if the rest of the area is the focus of more regular activity. An empty table with chairs arranged neatly around it can look rather bleak, generating a kind of waiting-room atmosphere. But there is no reason why the table should be left bare between meals or dinner parties. With only a little extra effort, it can be used as an additional place for arrangements: trays, platters and dishes piled with fruit, vases filled with flowers or collections of candlesticks – all of these can help to keep the area looking alive and lived-in.

Left and below Matthew Hilton candlesticks and Janice Tchalenko bowls dress the table between meals.

Left In front of an antique carved mirror an arrangement of flowers and fruit displays harmony of colour, form and scent: orchids in a tôle vase, beeswax candles, mangoes, Royal Gold lilies and hazelnut leaves in a Karen Bunting ceramic vase.

Above This simple arrangement celebrates the beauty of individual flowers of nerine and belladonna and the interesting leaf shapes of lemon-scented geranium picked from the garden. The table is covered with a folded linen cloth; beaten metal candlesticks are from a selection available at Designers Guild.

TABLE SETTINGS

Eating out at a good restaurant is like going to the theatre. Setting and presentation, colour, drama, and good company are all powerful elements that contribute to an enjoyable evening. These aspects of entertaining can be recreated at home, whether the event is a simple family meal or a formal dinner party.

A sense of occasion is easy to achieve. Essential ingredients include flowers and candles – elements that demand little effort but make an enormous difference. Presentation whets the appetite. Express enjoyment and create a welcoming atmosphere by choosing tablecloths, mats, napkins and crockery with an eye for

Above and right Sympathetic contrasts of colours and patterns add drama and vitality to table settings.

pattern and colour: appropriateness is important, as is the unexpected. I often use odd sets of four plates or bowls to set up unusual combinations.

INFORMAL USE

I always intended to preserve the garden view and the sense of connection with the outside, and this was one of the factors that influenced the decision not to separate the kitchen from the dining area in a more definitive way. Accordingly, there is an area in front of the French windows furnished with two armchairs. These are not a pair, but they sit well together. The chairs' loose covers, in simple white calico, are designed to be both easily removable for cleaning and also undemanding; their natural texture complements the other neutral colours in the room. With the light coming in from the south-facing garden, the different areas in the room are drawn together to create a cosy informality.

Like the odd pair of armchairs, the dining chairs are sympathetic in style but are not precise matches. Sets of dining chairs, whether contemporary or antique, can be fairly expensive; an alternative, but by no means a poor second choice, is to assemble a selection of individual chairs and enjoy the diversity. We searched out plain wooden upright chairs with straight backs and legs. All are Edwardian, a more functional and less ornamental period of design than Victorian. The chairs were stained charcoal and then grained to restore an impression of the natural quality and texture of the wood; the seats were upholstered in white calico. The decorative treatment unifies the set, but at the same time the slight variations of style and the 'skyline' of different heights provide a sense of wit and interest that can be lacking in rigidly symmetrical or matching arrangements. Such informality can be welcoming and hospitable.

Above and right At the garden end of the kitchen and dining room, French doors lead to the terrace. Comfortable armchairs, simply upholstered in plain white calico, promote an atmosphere of informality.

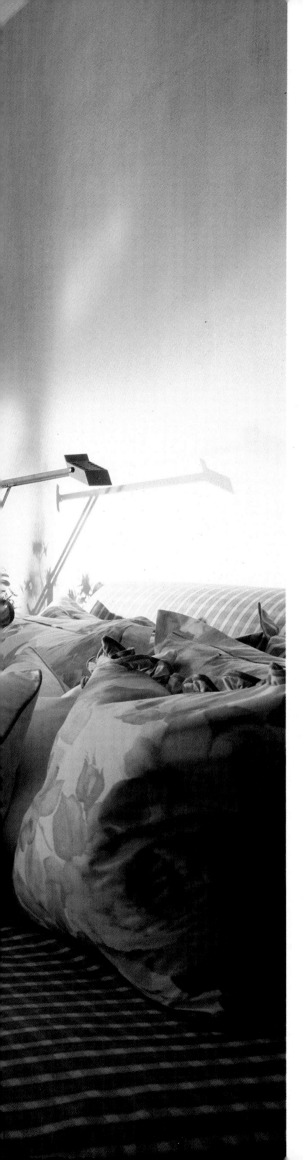

THE
MASTER
BEDROOM

The bedroom is where the first and last moments of the day are spent, so the atmosphere created in it through decoration and furnishing is very important. A bedroom should be comfortable, reasonably spacious, calm and intimate – a place of rest and refuge after a busy day.

Well-organized storage is the key to good bedroom design. Storage presents a real problem in most houses, and in the bedroom the need to find space for clothes, shoes and accessories can result in the room looking more like a cupboard with a bed in it than a peaceful retreat which is what it should be.

Remodelled from a series of small rooms on the second floor, the master bedroom is actually a suite of interconnected spaces, including walk-in clothes cupboards, a bathroom and a small lobby, as well as the bedroom itself. The way the available space was designed was determined first of all by storage requirements: the construction of separate storage areas allowed the bedroom to have its own identity.

BEDROOM LAYOUT

In older terraced or town houses it is fairly typical to find rooms of varying sizes at upper levels – often one large space, with one or more quite tiny adjacent rooms. Redesigning the layout – if there is an opportunity to do this – may result in a better use of space, one that is more in tune with today's requirements. In any case, it may be worth devoting one of the smaller rooms entirely to storage, freeing space in the bedroom and making it more habitable. An alternative, if the bedroom is fairly large, is to build a dividing wall and create a walk-in dressing area. In this way, clothes storage can be tailored precisely to your needs and the remaining bedroom area will have more character.

In our master bedroom, the feeling of space generated by its overall layout was emphasized by the new architectural detailing. The entrance to the suite of spaces is through double doors – taller and wider than the original entrance. Similarly, the connection between the bedroom and lobby is a large, square opening, creating through-views, and the connection between the bedroom and dressing area is also open, so that the third window along the wall can be seen. A mirror at the dressing-room entrance maximizes the natural light.

Below (left to right) A small lobby leads to the main bedroom area. From there, an open doorway connects to a walk-in dressing room lined with glass shelves, rails and drawers.

Above right An attractive arrangement of covered hat boxes.

There is always a temptation to fill space, but empty areas can have a very beneficial effect on architectural quality. The small square entrance lobby not only separates the spaces, but gives their whole sequence proportion and dignity.

Furniture layout in the bedroom is based on the position of the bed. There is often little option as to where the bed can go; however, if there is a choice, think about the advantages and disadvantages of different positions. Where will you gain the benefit of natural light and views from windows? Is it easy to make the bed? Is there a clear, unobstructed route to the door?

CLOTHES STORAGE

Practical storage means working out in detail what you need to store and then making the best use of available space. Think about your requirements – how much hanging space is needed, which items are used daily and which rarely, how much room is needed for accessories such as shoes, hats and handbags. Measure clothes: skirts, trousers and shirts will need half the hanging space of full-length coats and dresses.

Fitted cupboards are rarely attractive. They dominate a bedroom and can be wasteful of space; also, the areas at the top are often under-used, while clutter tends to accumulate at the bottom. By contrast, the type of storage and display found in modern clothes shops can be a good source of ideas. Basically open, with fitted shelves and rails, this design is extremely practical and efficient, but regular dusting is important.

The dressing areas in the master bedroom are designed so that each wall is fitted with a combination of rails, shelves and drawers. The partition walls are made of MDF (medium-density fibreboard). Between these rather structural uprights are compartments organized to provide different types of clothes storage. Shelves for clothes that fold flat are made of industrial-weight glass and rest on black brackets (in fact drawer handles) – a neat and stylish detail. These shelves have a light, clean appearance, and it is possible to see at a glance what is there. Drawers with glass fronts are used to store small items, and there are shelves placed at a high level to accommodate clothes that are rarely worn. Hanging space is organized so that there is both double hanging, with the upper rail set at the limit of arm's reach, and single hanging for full-length clothes.

Twice a year, there is a major seasonal reorganization, when, for example, winter clothes are put away and summer clothes arranged in their place. This not only helps clothes to last longer but also saves space.

More traditional types of storage can also be found in the bedroom. I enjoy the old-fashioned quality of wardrobes and chests of drawers; their design and patina add to the style of the room. Hatboxes are another attractive and practical type of storage; they remain by far the best way of keeping hats in good condition. Piled up in a collection and covered with fabric, they make a decorative pattern and shape.

DECORATION AND FURNISHING

Unlike the living room, where the decoration evolved out of the decision to use a particular fabric, the starting point in the bedroom was the colour of the walls. Green is a colour that can take on many different characters, depending on its precise shade and the way that it is used. Rich greens, which contain a high proportion of blue, can make vibrant and elegant backgrounds, as in the case of the living room. But here the colour is fresher and more yellow – still a striking contrast to the blue of the hall, but, as this is a bedroom, lighter and more restful. To maintain the sense of lightness and space, the carpet is of goats' hair cord in a natural white.

After the wall colour was decided, a mixture of patterned fabrics was selected. For the blinds we chose *Damask Rose*, a large flower print of roses on a yellow background. Matching this pattern in strength, *Streamer* was used to upholster the bed. This small blue check print has a contrasting scale and mood, but a small amount of yellow in the stripe relates back to the blind fabric, creating an underlying affinity. In the same

way, the blinds are edged in blue, relating to the predominant colour of the bed fabric. The other principal fabric is *Acanthus*, a pattern based on acanthus leaves but combined with a check so that it has a formal, classical quality.

Building on the basic pattern mixture, there are many pillows and cushions, covered in a range of fabrics, together with fabric-covered hatboxes and checked blankets. Additional colour is provided by bedside rugs, which serve also to protect the carpet where it receives most wear.

Above left The bed, upholstered in *Streamer* and piled high with cushions in the daytime, is the focal point of the room.

Above right An armchair covered in *Acanthus*.

The bed, although reminiscent of the typical Biedermeier sleigh bed in shape, was specially designed and intended to be upholstered. I like upholstered beds – they have a tailored appearance which means that the bedroom becomes a comfortable place to sit and read during the daytime.

If one important rule of pattern mixing is to set up a series of colour relationships, another is to provide mediating areas so that the room does not become over-upholstered, confusing or discordant. As well as the plain white carpet, visual breathing space is created by the white glazed-cotton upholstery of some of the chairs and stools, and by the presence of antique wooden furniture. Most of these pieces have the restrained classical appearance of the Biedermeier period of design, but the wood is generally richer than the blond finish traditionally associated with this style. The table in the seating area in front of the windows is in *faux* bamboo.

There is no reason to treat both bedsides in the same way: it can be interesting as well as practical to furnish them differently. On one side, there is a pink-spattered painted table, with a collection of objects, flowers and books; on the other there is a chest of drawers, with personal objects and photographs placed on top.

The juxtaposition of old and new furniture with plain and patterned fabrics, creates a pleasing palette of textures and patterns, adding to the decorative rhythm of the master bedroom.

Above and below right An alternative to the imposed symmetry of matching bedside tables is to treat each side of the bed in a different manner. Here an antique chest of drawers on the right side of the bed contrasts with a modern painted table on the right.

Right Each surface holds arrangements of flowers, photographs and books, together with a modern Italian angled light for bedside reading.

THE MASTER BATHROOM

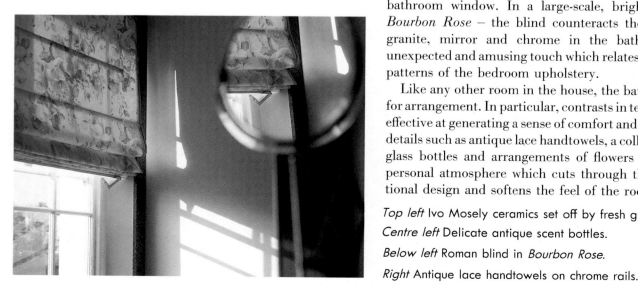

Like the kitchen, the bathroom is an intensely practical room. There is the need to accommodate built-in fittings in a workable sequence, demands for storage and special lighting requirements. Bathrooms should be safe and easy to keep clean; surfaces should be water-resistant.

But to design a bathroom concentrating solely on function is to ignore an important element. Bathrooms are also about comfort; they should be enjoyable as well as efficient, decorated as well as designed. If at all possible, they should be treated as extensions of the bedroom, linked by common colours or themes.

One way to achieve this, if space permits, is to separate the lavatory and bidet from the rest of the bathroom, either by building an enclosure or cubicle, or by putting a partition wall between the lavatory and the bathtub and basins. This type of layout means that privacy is no longer essential in the main bathroom area and it can consequently be integrated more closely with the bedroom.

This bathroom, across the small lobby from the master bedroom, has been designed to echo the decorative themes of the rest of the house. Contemporary, with clean, graphic lines, the design is classical rather than high-tech in inspiration. Surfaces are clad in black and white granite inset with the same square motif displayed on all the new architectural detailing. The floor consists of rectangular terrazzo tiles in two colours. Generous mirrors over the double basins (a good idea if two people are using the same bathroom) press shut over storage cabinets inset 10cm (4in) into the wall. Accessories – taps, towels, rails, door handles, radiator grilles – are chrome; some new, some salvaged from a 1930s building.

These crisp, hard-edged surfaces make a strong contrast to the soft, upholstered finish of the bedroom. But linking the two areas together is the exuberant Roman blind at the bathroom window. In a large-scale, bright floral print – *Bourbon Rose* – the blind counteracts the severity of the granite, mirror and chrome in the bathroom. It is an unexpected and amusing touch which relates back to the floral patterns of the bedroom upholstery.

Like any other room in the house, the bathroom is a place for arrangement. In particular, contrasts in texture can be very effective at generating a sense of comfort and enjoyment. Here details such as antique lace handtowels, a collection of delicate glass bottles and arrangements of flowers help to create a personal atmosphere which cuts through the serious, functional design and softens the feel of the room.

Top left Ivo Mosely ceramics set off by fresh green foliage.

Centre left Delicate antique scent bottles.

Below left Roman blind in *Bourbon Rose*.

Right Antique lace handtowels on chrome rails.

CUSHION COVERS

You can scatter ripples of colour and pattern over a bed or sofa to great effect by alternating solid-coloured cushions that have a contrast piping with ones made from different types of fabric. To achieve a luxuriously plump look, make sure that your cushion pads measure 2.5cm (1in) more each way than the covers, excluding frills. Two cushion designs are shown here – one with a bound frill and one with a flat frill.

BOUND FRILL COVER

To make a cover to fit a 54cm ($21\frac{1}{2}$in) square pad, you will need fabric 140cm (56in) wide, cut as follows: 60cm (24in) of main fabric, 20cm (8in) of fabric for frill, 10cm (4in) of fabric for frill edge, plus matching threads and a 46cm (18in) zip.

Cut a 54cm ($21\frac{1}{2}$in) square for the front (notch the central point on one side), and two backs, each 28.5cm × 54cm ($11\frac{1}{4}$in × $21\frac{1}{2}$in). With right sides facing, tack the backs together and stitch at each end – 4cm ($1\frac{1}{2}$in) for bound frill, 7cm ($2\frac{3}{4}$in) for flat frill – leaving zip opening tacked. Press seam flat. Whipstitch zip tapes together above the top; pin and tack zip face-down over back cover, centring the teeth over the seamline. With right side of back uppermost, topstitch zip in place, stitching 1.5cm ($\frac{1}{2}$in) from seamline all along each side. Remove tacking.

For the frill, cut three strips across the width of the fabric, each 4cm ($1\frac{1}{2}$in) wide, and three edge strips, each 2cm ($\frac{3}{4}$in) wide. Join frill strips into a circle using French seams – with wrong sides facing and a 3mm ($\frac{1}{8}$in) seam allowance, stitch together; fold right side out and stitch again, taking a 6mm ($\frac{1}{4}$in) allowance and enclosing raw edges. Join the edge strips with plain 1.5cm ($\frac{1}{2}$in) seams.

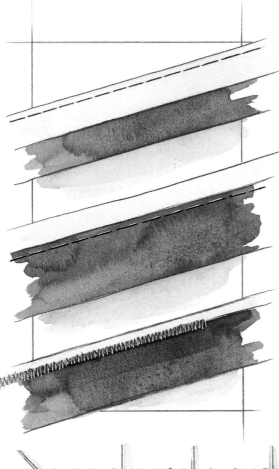

Join the right side of the edge strip to the wrong side of the frill, taking a 3mm ($\frac{1}{8}$in) seam allowance. Press seam towards edge strip, then fold this to the right side of the frill, just covering the seam. Satin stitch in place. Run two lines of gathering around raw edge of frill.

With bound edge inwards, lay frill on front cover, pinning and gathering to fit (place pins at right angles to the seamline). Stitching 1.5cm ($\frac{1}{2}$in) from raw edges, sew frill to front cover. With right sides facing and enclosing the frill, stitch the back of the cushion to the front (leave zip open). Reinforce the corners then cut away the seam allowances, cutting across at a diagonal, to make turning easier. Turn cover right side out.

FLAT FRILL COVER

To make a cover to fit a 50cm (20in) square pad, you will need 60cm (24in) of fabric 140cm (56in) wide, two contrast threads for satin stitching, matching thread and a 46cm (18in) zip. Cut one front 59cm (23$\frac{1}{2}$in) square (make a notch at the central point on one side) and two backs, each 31cm × 59cm (12$\frac{1}{4}$in × 23$\frac{1}{2}$in).

Make the back as described for the bound frill cushion and, with zip open, stitch the back cover to the front cover. Clip corners, turn through to right side and press. With a pencil and ruler, draw a square 4cm (1$\frac{1}{2}$in) in from the cushion edge. Tack, then satin stitch along this line (start stitching halfway along one line to avoid puckers at the corners). Make the inner row of satin stitching 6mm ($\frac{1}{4}$in) away from the first row.

FABRIC-COVERED BOXES

Fabric boxes are a practical way of adding colour, form and texture to a room and at the same time, avoiding clutter. For maximum effect, make several boxes, using a range of patterns and colours that complement those used for the other soft furnishings of the room. In the main bedroom, for instance, two hatboxes at the foot of the bed are covered in the same pattern as the bed itself, one of them in a contrasting colourway to the main fabric.

The diagrams show how to make a square-topped box which is covered with lightly padded fabric and contains an inner lining.

As an alternative to making your own box you can buy a ready-made card hatbox and glue the fabric in place. To do this, first measure the depth and circumference of the box and the lid. Cut out pieces of fabric to the circumference length plus a 6mm ($\frac{1}{4}$in) overlap, and to the depth minus 3mm ($\frac{1}{8}$in) at top and bottom of the box.

Using the box lid, make a paper template. Place the template on the

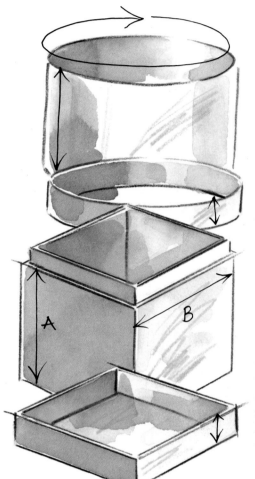

fabric and cut out the lid shape. Trim this fabric to lie just short of the lid's edge.

Depending on the fabric used, it may be best to seal fraying edges with roller blind stiffener before gluing the fabric pieces to the box.

If you wish to use a fabric with a large motif, base the size of the box on the size of the pattern repeats in the fabric so that a motif appears on each face of the box as well as on the lid.

SQUARE-TOPPED BOX

To make a square-topped box with an inner lining and a 2.5cm (1in) deep lid, cut four sides from mediumweight card measuring A (desired height less 2.5cm [1in]) × B (width of box sides) and four pieces of domett the same size. Using display mount, fix the pieces, dommett side down, to the wrong side of a strip of fabric, leaving 3mm ($\frac{1}{8}$in) between each piece of card and a margin of 1.5cm ($\frac{1}{2}$in) of fabric all around. Fold the fabric neatly over the card. Glue the sides first and then along the top and bottom. Bring the sides together and slip stitch.

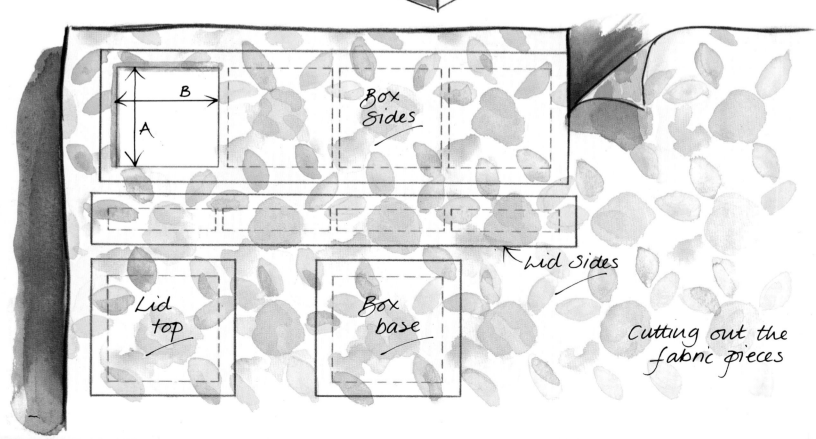

Box Sides

Lid Sides

Lid top

Box base

Cutting out the fabric pieces

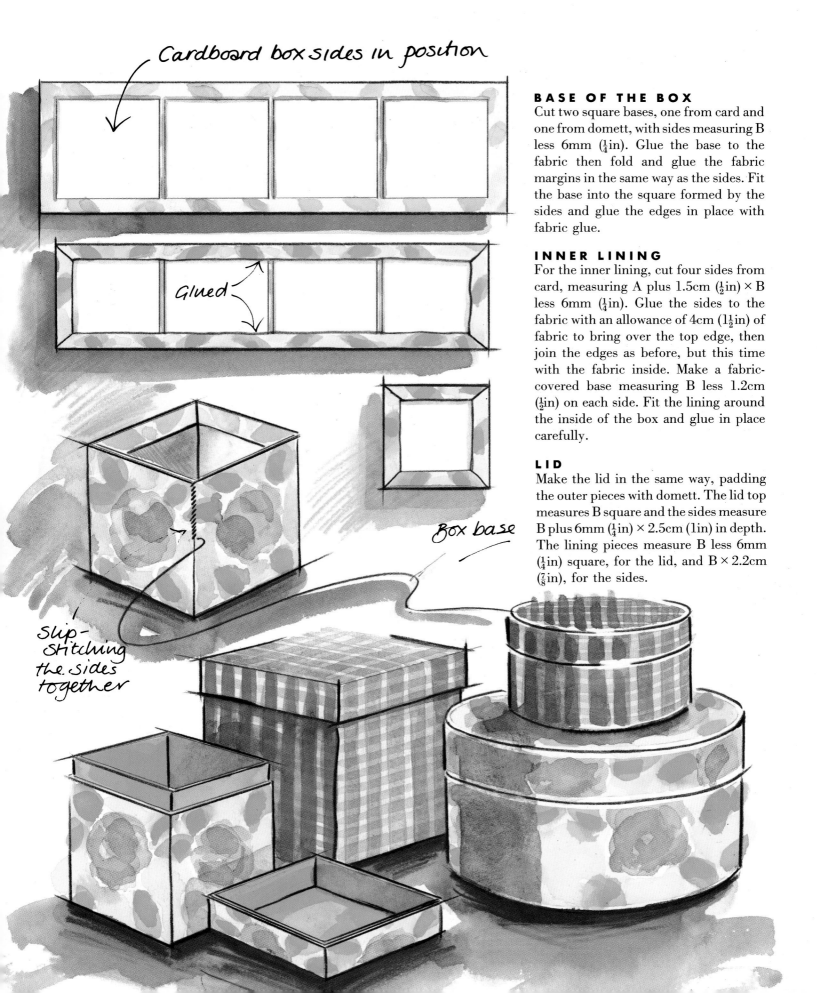

Cardboard box sides in position

Glued

slip-stitching the sides together

Box base

BASE OF THE BOX

Cut two square bases, one from card and one from domett, with sides measuring B less 6mm ($\frac{1}{4}$in). Glue the base to the fabric then fold and glue the fabric margins in the same way as the sides. Fit the base into the square formed by the sides and glue the edges in place with fabric glue.

INNER LINING

For the inner lining, cut four sides from card, measuring A plus 1.5cm ($\frac{1}{2}$in) × B less 6mm ($\frac{1}{4}$in). Glue the sides to the fabric with an allowance of 4cm ($1\frac{1}{2}$in) of fabric to bring over the top edge, then join the edges as before, but this time with the fabric inside. Make a fabric-covered base measuring B less 1.2cm ($\frac{1}{2}$in) on each side. Fit the lining around the inside of the box and glue in place carefully.

LID

Make the lid in the same way, padding the outer pieces with domett. The lid top measures B square and the sides measure B plus 6mm ($\frac{1}{4}$in) × 2.5cm (1in) in depth. The lining pieces measure B less 6mm ($\frac{1}{4}$in) square, for the lid, and B × 2.2cm ($\frac{7}{8}$in), for the sides.

THE TERRACOTTA BEDROOM

Bedrooms are personal places; each should be individual. By tradition, they tend to be treated in a rather feminine manner, with fabric used extensively for upholstery, curtains and bed dressing to create an enveloping sense of softness and comfort.

This room, designed and decorated for my daughter, displays all the common themes that form the basis of the decoration throughout the house: strong colour, graphic, contemporary detail, and pattern mixing. But the room has an airy feeling, a sense of light and space, that gives it a personality of its own. And, although it is essentially a feminine room in terracotta and white, the black details are very important, adding crispness and strength.

The four-poster in this room provides the opportunity to display fabric and generate a sense of warmth and enclosure, adding another dimension to the bed, and giving it an interior of its own. The bed curtains, which are made from the same fabric as that used for the Roman blind help to create the sense of a room-within-a-room.

DECORATION

Peach – flattering, warm and subtle – is a shade that has been enthusiastically adopted in modern interiors. It covers a wide range of tones, from pale pastel orangey pinks, that can be insipid and bland, to a deeper terracotta colour with more character.

The rich earthiness of terracotta pots was the inspiration for the wall colour in this room. Originally we selected a lighter shade, but this was deepened and strengthened during the process of painting the walls: seeing the initial colour against the intensity of the blue hall prompted the change. Although there is not a great difference in tone between the wall colour and the colour of the bed curtains, the fact that the walls are slightly deeper and richer prevents the decoration from looking too soft.

This is essentially a coordinated room, with important exceptions. The main fabric, used to make the bed curtains and Roman blinds, is an abstract design, one of a small collection handpainted by Caroline Grey for Designers Guild. The material displays a slightly lighter tone of the terracotta used on the walls, and its painterly quality goes well with them. With the bedcover, the curtain linings and the upholstery of a chair and stool in simple white glazed cotton, and with the natural white cord carpet on the floor, the room has a great feeling of light and space as well as warmth.

Contrast, however, is particularly crucial in this room, especially the use of black. Table lights, picture frames, bedside tables and the metal rods and rings on the four-poster bed are all black, adding definition to the soft, coordinated scheme. An armchair, upholstered in another handpainted fabric, is a surprising, clear blue – a vivid contrast that links with the blue of the hall.

DRESSING A BED

In the past, the bed was an extremely important piece of furniture. The ancestor of the four-poster – the tester bed with its canopy and curtains – was designed to provide privacy and warmth. But in grand houses in particular, these monumental beds were also symbols of status and wealth; their drapery was often intricate and highly ornate.

Today there is a tendency for the bed to be rather less of a focal point. Low divan beds, without headboards or drapery, have a plain functional look that may suit certain types of interiors. But, whatever its form, a bed takes up a good proportion of space in a room and to ignore its decorative potential is to miss a valuable opportunity.

A four-poster bed can help to bring back a sense of style and drama – but this type of design need not invariably be nostalgic. The four-poster beds in the house, from Designers Guild, consist of square-sectioned wooden uprights fixed to the floor and linked at the top by a simple framework of metal rods. Depending on the way the wooden posts are finished and on the style of drapery, the overall effect can be rich and luxurious, contemporary or romantic.

The bedposts are painted in shades of white and grey – not glossy and even, but in a distressed matt finish. The curtains, two at each corner, are gathered and suspended from black metal rings. Falling right onto the floor, but not overly full, they have a classic look, suggesting columns. And the modern fabric, edged with white lining turned over as banding, pursues the contemporary theme.

Left A glowing watercolour by William Tillyer from a series painted in the Mediterranean. Poppies and euphorbia in a ceramic vase, wooden boxes and a leather-bound book emphasize the warmth and richness of the decoration.

Right Sunlight slants across a side table piled with handpainted wooden boxes – decorated versions of a plain Shaker design. Bright yellow Michaelmas daisies and solidago in a blue pot add a jolt of vivid colour.

BED CURTAINS

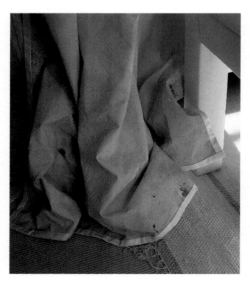

Traditionally, bed curtains performed the highly important function of keeping out cold draughts. Nowadays, however, they are used simply as a decorative feature, to create a feeling of comfort and luxury, and offer a chance to add to a decorative scheme further pattern and texture as well as a feeling of softness. The four-poster beds in the guest room and the terracotta bedroom each have bed hangings consisting of eight curtains – two at the head, two at the foot, and two at each side of the bed. Each curtain measures only one fabric-width across and is loosely but generously gathered, so that the pairs of curtains cannot in fact be drawn fully together. If they had been made wide enough to be closed over, they would have looked bunched-up when drawn back, losing the general effect of elegant columns of fabric draped at each corner of the bed.

DECORATIVE POSSIBILITIES

Bed curtains offer great decorative possibilities; it is enjoyable to spend time planning the style of the curtains and choosing the right fabrics and trimmings to echo and reinforce the feeling of the room as a whole. Loosely gathered sheer fabrics give an impression of lightness and femininity; beads and fringing may be used for an exotic look.

Bed curtains are made in much the same way as window curtains, the important difference being that the lining – that is, the side facing in towards the bed – is as much on view as the fabric on the outside. This offers a splendid opportunity for attractive contrasts, like that between the large-scale *Waterleaf* pattern and the check-printed lining, *Tracery*, of the bed curtains in the guest room. Similarly, the fabric of the curtain lining should look as neat and attractive as the outside, so a bound edging, that looks equally finished on both sides, is more attractive than a conventional hem.

The method you use for gathering likewise requires some thought.

Although bought heading tape may be a convenient way to gather curtains, it is not particularly attractive when viewed from the back, and even on the front the lines of machine stitching may slightly mar the overall effect. Another disadvantage of ordinary heading tape is that the range of gathers available is limited by the number of designs on sale. For these reasons, the curtains for the four-poster beds in my house were gathered by hand and the rings were sewn in place to a tape formed from the same fabric that had been used for the lining.

TECHNIQUE

To create curtains like these, first measure the curtain fabric so that the bottom 15cm (6in) lies on the floor, rather than hanging clear of it, and allow also a stand of 7.5cm (3in) above the point at which the rings will be attached. Using the full width of the fabric in each case, cut the main fabric and lining of each curtain to the finished length. For each curtain cut two edging strips from the lining fabric, each 6cm (2¼in) deep and the full width of the fabric. Again from the lining fabric, cut a strip 12.5cm (5in) deep and the full width of the fabric. Remove selvedges and trim the main fabric to make it 6cm (2¼in) narrower than the lining fabric. To stiffen the top of the curtain, cut a strip of iron-on, heavyweight dressmaker's interfacing, 10cm (4in) deep and the width of the main fabric. Position it 1.5cm (½in) down from the top raw edge of the main fabric and iron it in place.

With raw edges and right sides together, join the lining and the main fabric together down the sides, taking 1.5cm (½in) seams. Turn the resulting tube of fabric right side out and press, so that an even 1.5cm (½in) edging of lining fabric can be seen at each side of the main fabric. Take the edging strips and, on each strip, fold in the long edges by 1.5cm (½in) and press; then bring the folded edges together and press again.

Fold out the first strip and, with right sides and raw edges together and leaving an even overlap at each side, attach the strip to the right side of the top of the curtain, stitching through all layers of fabric and taking a 1.5cm ($\frac{1}{2}$in) seam allowance. Turn in the short edges, bring the strip over to the wrong/lining side, and stitch it in place by hand. Edge the bottom of the curtain in the same way.

Working by hand, gather the top of the curtain, making two lines of gathering stitches, one 7cm ($2\frac{3}{4}$in) below the top of the curtain, and another about 2cm ($\frac{3}{4}$in) lower. Make sure that as little stitching as possible is visible on the right side of the curtain. Draw up the gathering threads and tie them off. Space the gathers evenly.

Trim the remaining lining strip to the gathered curtain width. Turn in short ends, then bring over the long raw edges to meet. Fold over and press, enclosing raw edges. By hand or machine, stitch the folded edges together. Pin the folded strip to the curtain lining, covering the gathering stitches. Slipstitch it in place by hand, so that no stitches show on the right side of the curtain. Finally, sew curtain rings to the strip at regular 7.5cm (3in) intervals.

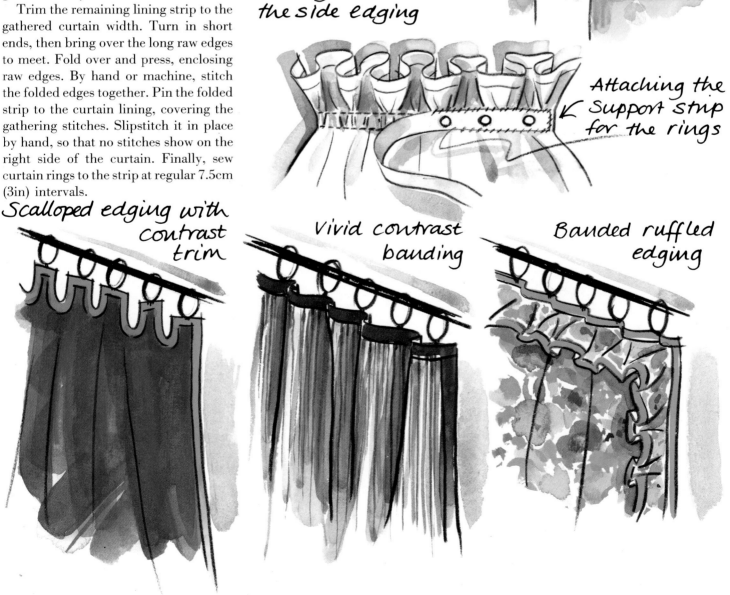

Lining fabric forms the side edging

Attaching the support strip for the rings

Scalloped edging with contrast trim

Vivid contrast banding

Banded ruffled edging

THE TERRACOTTA BATHROOM

Decorated in the same peach and black, the bathroom is linked to the bedroom by a small hallway fitted with shelves and rails to act as a dressing room. The handmade bathroom tiles, with their random finish, have a softness and depth that echoes the paint finish in the bedroom and helps to unify the two rooms. As in the bedroom, black is an important element. It is used to provide definition and contrast: black Venetian blinds, black metal towel rail and pivoting circular mirrors above the sink framed in black.

By coordinating colour and detail, you can transform ordinary objects into an enjoyable arrangement. Here, soft peach towels hanging from black rails make a contrast of texture, form and colour – a functional arrangement that can also be appreciated for its decorative effect. The addition of natural foliage in a simple rectangular glass vase and brightly-coloured ceramics on and around the bath adds another dimension to the decorative scheme, softening it and also providing a sense of welcome.

Top left Black-framed pivoting mirrors have a sculptural quality.

Top right Two ceramic dishes by Carol McNichol and a splash of green foliage.

Above left Wrapped soap from Molton Brown adds a touch of luxury.

Above right and above Against the unity of the randomly finished handmade tiles, the black metal towel rail lends definition.

THE GUEST
ROOM
AND ATTIC ROOMS

A guest room is all too often simply a spare room where odds and ends tend to collect. Often there is mismatched furniture consisting of pieces that do not fit in elsewhere or simply need to be stored. But, if you have the space for a visitors' room, it is worth making it a really welcoming place.

When designing a guest room, a different set of ideas and needs come into play. Above all, the room should be comfortable and warm, a place in which visitors will enjoy staying. But most guest rooms are not very big, and they often have a poor aspect, which means they can be dark and cold. This room, which is small in floor area and faces north, is, unfortunately, no exception.

Given these limitations, the temptation might be to keep decoration and furnishing light and simple. However, rather than adopt this remedial approach, I decided to fill the room with colour and pattern, creating a strong sense of character with a touch of fantasy – a treatment that transcends the inherent problems.

PATTERN MIXING

In many ways, the decoration of the room breaks all the rules. In a single small space there are three different and intensely coloured patterns: one covering the walls, one for the upholstery and bed, and one for the curtains, the lining of the bed curtains and the bed cover. The four-poster bed itself is rather large for the space; the upholstered headboard is high. The carpet is of black cord, and everywhere you look there are vivid jolts of colour: pink and turquoise tables, turquoise banding and bright ceramics. The effect of all this intensity is to generate a sense of warmth and intimacy.

The success of the decoration depends on careful pattern mixing. If all the fabric in the room had been in the same pattern, the effect might well have been ordinary. Instead, the strong, rich colours and the blend of flower and geometric prints help to keep the room alive and full of interest. On the walls is a green and turquoise check print called *Streamer*, creating an effect slightly reminiscent of the Victorian penchant for covering walls in bright plaids. *Streamer* is used also on the upholstered stool in front of the narrow raspberry-pink painted table. The bed is hung with *Waterleaf*, a fluid, large-scale pattern in greens and blues. The interior of the bed, the high headboard, the window curtains and the lining of the bed are all in another check print, *Tracery*, in soft reds, greens, blues and yellows.

FABRIC ON WALLS

Covering walls with fabric creates a feeling of warmth and comfort, which is one reason why this treatment was chosen for the north-facing guest room. If you decide to use this type of covering for a room, careful planning is essential, whether you intend to put up the fabric yourself or employ a professional.

There are various ways of using fabric to cover walls, ranging from shirring fine fabric onto rods positioned at the top and bottom of the wall, to pasting prepared fabric directly onto it. The method used in the guest room, however, was firstly to screw laths to the wall then attach a thin layer of polyester wadding followed by the fabric itself.

A firm good-quality cotton is ideal for this treatment, in order to minimize the danger of stretching. An overall pattern is obviously much simpler to use than one with strong directional lines that have to be carefully matched up at joins.

Equally it is important to look very carefully at the architecture of the room and plan in detail which features you want to emphasize and which to play down. Also, decide whether doors should be covered or left as they are. If pictures are to be used on the walls, it must be decided in advance exactly where they will hang, so battens can be placed at those points.

EDGING

Another decision concerns the type of edging to be used. Edging strips will be needed to cover the tacks or staples that attach the fabric to the battens. Just as with piping on upholstery and cushions

(see pages 52–3), edging can be used to emphasize a particular feature, to add contrast, to tie the wall covering in with other elements of the decoration, or to disguise certain aspects of the room. In the guest room, for instance, the turquoise edging strip is made from the same fabric as the edging of the bed curtains, and its bright, vivid colour adds to the warmth and liveliness of the room. However, there is a supporting beam at the top of one wall: a turquoise edging around the lower edge of this beam would have drawn attention to it. In order to avoid this, the edging covering the join between the beam and the rest of the wall is made from the same fabric as the wall covering, so that it blends in unobtrusively.

Braid or other purchased trims can be used, but it is very easy to prepare your own edging. To make an edging 1.5cm ($\frac{1}{2}$in) wide, cut a 3.5cm ($1\frac{1}{4}$in) strip from the chosen fabric, trimming away selvedges. Where necessary, join lengths together with straight seams. If you are making a large quantity of edging you may find that it helps to first measure and cut a long strip of card to the correct width for use as a template. When you have cut and joined sufficient strips, press in the raw edges on each long side, with wrong sides together, so that the folded edges overlap by 5mm ($\frac{1}{4}$in). Using matching thread and a machine straight stitch, sew down the centre of the folded strip. It is now ready to be glued in position, covering raw edges and staples.

Covering walls in fabric is generally more difficult than straightforward pa-

pering, but even if you do not wish to use fabric for the walls, it may be used to cover doors – for example, wardrobe doors such as those in the guest room. Either cover the entire surface or leave space for a frame of wood, about 10cm (4in) deep, around the outer edges.

TECHNIQUE

To cover a flush door, first measure the length and width of the door. Take the door off its hinges so that it can be laid flat for ease of working, and remove the handle, if any. If there is a frame, draw the inner line in pencil on the door, to act as a guide for the measurements. Cut polyester wadding and fabric to the required proportions, and staple first the wadding and then the fabric to the door, stapling at the edges. Work outwards from the central point at the top and bottom edges and then do the same at the sides, making sure that the fabric is evenly stretched and exactly matches the door's edges (or the marked lines, if you are planning to have a wooden frame). You may find it simpler to use display mount rather than staples to fix the wadding in position.

If you are leaving a frame of wood around the fabric, pin and glue strips of wood moulding, approximately 1.5cm ($\frac{1}{2}$in) wide, along the marked frame lines, mitring the corners. Paint the moulding and the outer wooden frame if desired, and then complete the door by gluing the fabric edging strips in position, to cover the staples. Finally, when all the fabric is evenly applied to the surface, reattach the door handle.

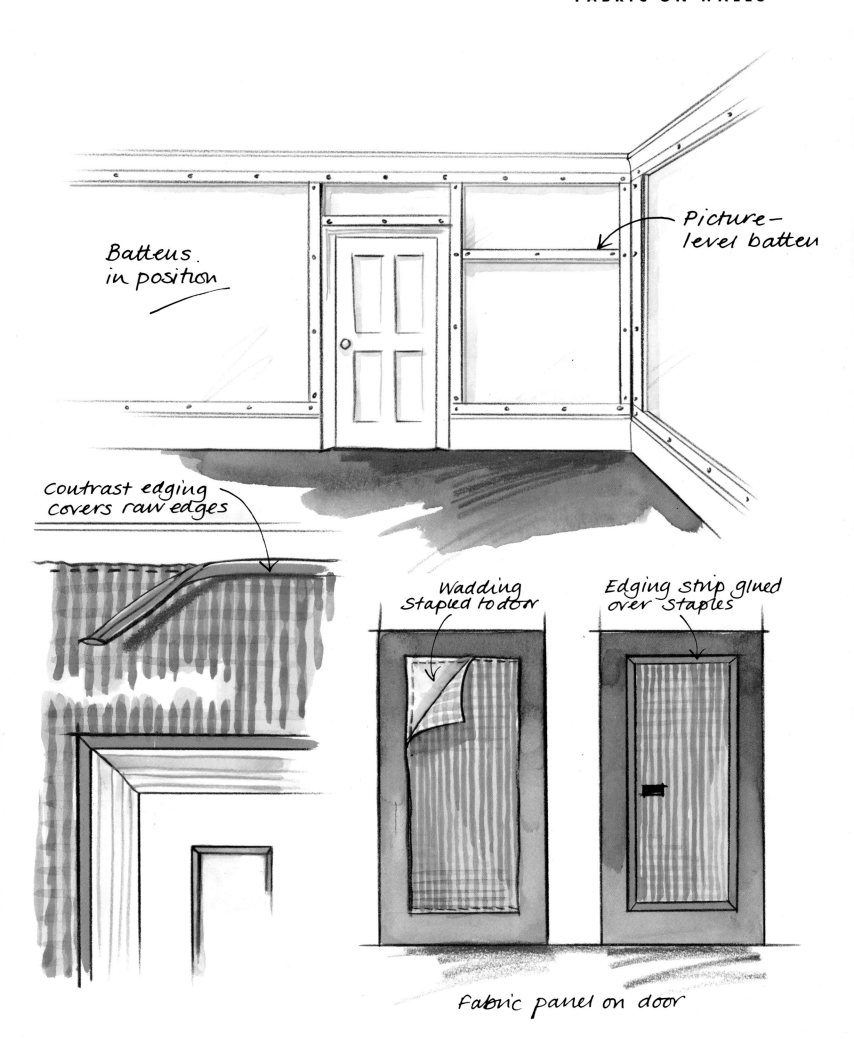

Picture-level batten

Battens in position

Contrast edging covers raw edges

Wadding stapled to door

Edging strip glued over staples

fabric panel on door

THE GUEST BATHROOM

Directly adjoining the bedroom, the guest bathroom is a tiny room where there is only just enough space to accommodate all the necessary fittings. Because it is a small area, but can be seen from the bedroom, it is all in one colour: the same vivid turquoise used in the bedroom to highlight and draw together the different patterns. Viewed from the bedroom, this glimpse of vibrant colour has the same effect as the banding and other turquoise details of the room.

As in the terracotta bathroom, the tiles are handmade and randomly finished, which prevents the single-colour scheme from looking flat. There is a large mirror on one wall which helps to make the room seem more spacious. To avoid introducing another colour or pattern which might induce a cluttered atmosphere in such a small space, the window is covered with a plain white Roman blind edged in black.

To soften the hard, reflective surfaces of colour, brightly coloured informal flowers and hung towels are useful additions. The deep green towels provide an unexpected colour contrast.

Left Bright turquoise, used to throw the rich patterns of the guest room into relief, is the predominant colour in the adjoining bathroom.

Top French Art Nouveau glass vase.

Above Soap in a shallow soap dish.

THE ATTIC ROOMS

At the top of the house are two small rooms, one of which has been furnished to provide a study for my daughter, the other as a second guest bedroom. Because these rooms are located right under the roof, they have deep dormer windows, odd angles and sloping ceilings. The particular challenge was to make positive use of these awkward shapes and proportions. Both rooms are papered in designs from the *Gesso* collection of traditionally printed wallpapers and borders inspired by frescoes. Here they simulate the effect of the paint finish used elsewhere in the house.

In an attic room or converted loft with a sloping ceiling, there is invariably an area where the ceiling is so low that the floor space beneath is unusable. In this room, the space has been filled with thick shelving that runs from wall to wall to take books, magazines, cassettes and records, leaving the rest of the room free from unsightly clutter.

The wallpaper borders in these rooms offer a good example of the way in which details can add impact. Like piping, borders can be strong and vivid, because their surface area is so small when compared with other elements of your design. The peacock-blue border in the attic study, for example, inspired by classical motifs, makes an interesting contrast with the walls.

In rooms like the two in this attic, which have sloping ceilings and other architectural oddities, the very fact that a border can be used to emphasize certain features makes it possible to play down other, less attractive aspects of the structure. Outlining the window and taking the borders along the skirting board in the bedroom, for example, draws the eye away from the angle of the ceiling.

Above Deeply recessed window in the attic study, outlined with *Cariola*, a peacock-blue border. *Right* Sofa upholstered in *Giardino*, a damask.

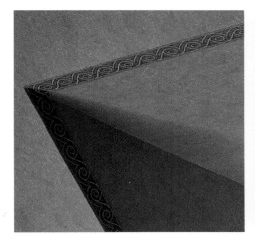

Left The attic study is papered in *Stucco*, enclosing the space in intense colour and providing depth and texture. The same vivid green of the sofa upholstery also occurs in the blind fabric, *Acanthus*. The other predominant colour is black — black coir on the floor, black background in the sofa fabric, black edging for the blinds and the black desk. A Clarice Cliff pot used as a pencil jar and a Fiestaware jug provide vivid points of interest.

Above The window recess and the planes and angles of the walls and ceiling are accentuated by the use of wallpaper borders from the *Gesso* collection.

THE ATTIC BEDROOM

In the little guest room next door, the wallpaper is *Leaf Fresco*, which has a traditional damask design in pale claret red superimposed on a warm yellow-and-rust textural background. The two colours vibrate slightly in juxtaposition; the pattern is muted rather than obvious. Covering a ceiling with a paper that has a large regular pattern repeat is usually not recommended, but in this case the design

Below An informal arrangement of bowls and vases, part of a china collection.

Right Tiny wrought-iron bed.

is subtle enough that the places where the repeats do not match are not glaringly obvious. Two borders, *Cariola* and *Treccia*, define the angles and planes of the walls, making a virtue out of what could have been an awkward space.

Traditionally used at the top of papered walls to conceal the trimmed edges, borders are in fact much more versatile than this. Borders will help to give a papered room definition and strengthen its architectural detailing; one way to emphasize this effect is to pair a wider border with a narrower one, as in

the attic bedroom. Here the two borders run in tandem – the narrower one above the wider one, with a small gap between – above the skirting board and the door and along the sloping angles of the dormer windows.

Against the background of black coir flooring a bright rag rug makes a stamp of colour. The wrought-iron bed is also black; a collection of lustreware on top of the chest of drawers contributes glowing colour. The mixture of a bold flower print, and a lime-and-grey striped blind and chair add individuality and welcome.

WALLPAPER BORDERS

In addition to stressing or muting architectural features, borders can be used in their own right to create new detailing. A wide border in a room with disproportionately high walls can stand in place of a cornice or picture rail and have the same effect of making the wall seem lower. Another option is to position a border at dado-rail height, with contrasting wallpapers above and below. A very long or a too tall room can be made to look better proportioned if panels of borders are used at intervals to break up the wall-space.

Whether the wall on which the border is to be hung is painted or papered, it is important that the surface should be thoroughly dry. Also, any deviation from the horizontal will show very clearly; as ceilings and cornices are often slightly out of true, it is essential to check them and, if necessary, to draw in an accurate horizontal. To do this, first find out how deep the border is and then measure down the wall to the point where the border's base-line will lie; add 2cm (¾in) to allow for possible adjustments. Repeat the process at several points along the wall, and then lightly pin a batten to the

wall, so that it joins together the marked points. Use a spirit level on the batten to determine that the line is horizontal. After you have adjusted the line where necessary, mark it with a pencil or by snapping chalked string against the wall.

The same basic technique can be used to create a border panel. Draw the outline of the inner border frame in position on the wall, using a spirit level to check the horizontal lines and a plumbline for the vertical lines.

To hang a horizontal border, align the lower edge with the guideline that is already marked. If hanging a long strip, paste it and then fold it into a concertina, so that you can release it a little at a time. Smooth the border in position with a brush, then use a seam roller, working sideways, to make sure that the border is well stuck down.

If it is necessary to join two lengths (perhaps the roll has come to an end), butt the cut ends up against each other, If there is a strong design, try to make the join where it will be least obvious: One way is to cut around the outlines of a design element such as a flower, so that you can jigsaw-fit the two ends of border.

Where two strips join at an angle, it is worth taking care to get the most attractive effect. One way to make a straightforward right-angled join is to make a mitre cut at a 45-degree angle at the end of each strip before pasting. Alternatively, apply the pasted strips to the wall so that they overlap each other. Before pressing them in position with the seam roller, lay a straightedge diagonally between the inner and the outer vertexes of the corner and cut along it with a craft knife. Peel away the overlapped pieces, leaving the mitred corner. This method can be used for any angle of join, not just a right-angle.

For a curved join, make a series of narrow V-shaped cuts, as shown in the illustration, until enough cuts have been made to achieve the correct degree of curve. Six 15-degree cuts, for example, will produce a right-angled curve.

Before you start making an angle, it is worth experimenting with the border to see what would look most attractive. In our attic rooms, for example, the strips, instead of being trimmed into curves or mitres, are laid across each other to create a less predictable effect.

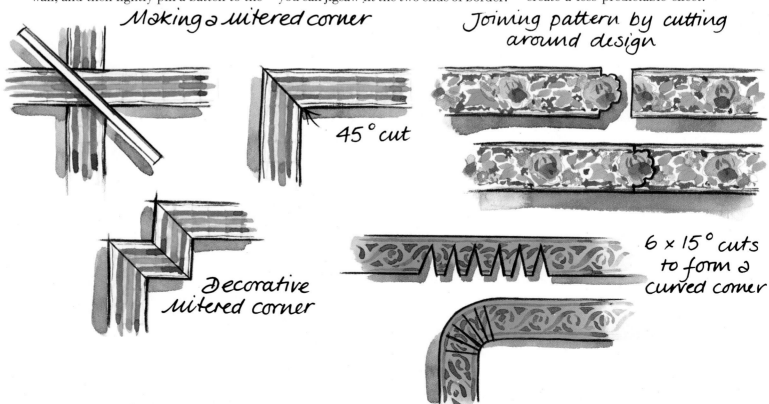

Making a mitered corner

45° cut

Joining pattern by cutting around design

Decorative mitered corner

6 x 15° cuts to form a curved corner

Border used to create paneled effect

Combining borders to accentuate a cornice

Single border above baseboard

wide border used to visually lower ceiling

Border at cornice level to balance

Border used as dado-rail

Border used to break up blank wall areas

Border used to frame doorway

THE
GARDEN

Like a room, a garden is fundamentally a space that should be planned, decorated and furnished with an eye for structure, colour, texture and form. However, unlike a room, a garden demands constant care if it is to continue to flourish. The climate in Britain, notoriously unpredictable and so frequently wet, can prevent the British from viewing their gardens as true outdoor rooms, or enjoying them as extensions of the interior. But in our household, we breakfast and lunch outside whenever the weather permits, or take cushions to sit and read or simply to enjoy the garden.

The garden is planned as a sequence of linked spaces, at varying levels and with different vantage points. The French windows at the lower level connect the dining room to a paved court furnished with a circular table and set of chairs, a sheltered suntrap for outdoor eating. From this area, a flight of stairs leads up to the ground level and the pond with its raised stone surround and a wooden garden bench. From the living room, French windows open onto a balcony at the side of which a metal stairway, added during the alterations to the exterior of the house, descends into the garden.

PLANNING AND PLANTING

Unless a new garden is being planted, you will have to begin by assessing what to keep and what to eliminate, looking at the underlying structure to see how it can be improved and what potential it has for development. Gardening demands both patience and ruthlessness. Moving a plant that is growing perfectly well where it is, for the sake of the overall design, means that you may have to wait for another five years before it begins to flourish in its new position.

We inherited a typical town garden, with a few overgrown bushes, large lime trees and some flowering shrubs. Most town gardens suffer from the problem of dry shade; mature trees, although useful for screening views and softening the outlines of neighbouring buildings, can deprive plants growing beneath them of nutrients, moisture and light. Limes in particular have the added disadvantage that they constantly drop sticky secre-

tions. For this reason we decided to take out one of the large lime trees. Some of the more overgrown bushes were dug out, leaving a pair of weeping cherries, a wonderful grapevine, jasmine and honeysuckle, all of which help to give the garden a basic structure. A huge mahonia was removed because it was wrong for its site, and because garden colours were to be essentially a combination of blue, white, mauve and pink.

The new planting was designed to provide as much year-round colour as possible, and to include a variety of form and habit. Foliage is at least as important as flowers – strong, interesting leaf shapes maintain interest even when a plant is not in bloom. We planted maples, and robinia for its lime-green leaves. In the shaded area, there are massed hostas – perfect, low-growing, woodland plants, with leaves in a wide range of shapes and shades.

In the spring, colour in the garden comes from blue and white snowdrops and grape hyacinths; giving way in the early summer to blue iris, mauve clematis climbing in the trees and wisteria. In their turn, these are succeeded by white, purple and striped roses, alchemilla, with its lime-green flowers, hardy geraniums, pink and purple lupins and the clear blue of delphiniums.

All gardens, but particularly town gardens, should include plants growing in pots as well as bedded in the earth. I grow many different species of lily, and several varieties of thyme in pots, arranged like objects around the edge of the pond. To soften the lines of the crazy stone paving, sections were taken out and replaced with a selection of plants, including creeping thyme, saxifrage, clumps of campanula and rock plants. They were planted to overflow the stones and fill the gaps in between.

Far left Different types and sizes of container help to provide variety in a town garden and contrasts of scale and leaf shape are as important as planting for colour.

Left and above Gardens can be furnished with seats, tables and chairs to encourage their use as true outdoor rooms.

THE MEWS HOUSE

The typical London mews house, now desirable property, had humble origins as a stable or garage. Tucked away down narrow alleys or culs-de-sac, these terraced houses have become extremely fashionable pieds-à-terre now their original function is largely redundant.

In total floor area, most mews houses equal the size of an average flat or small maisonette but, unlike apartments, their particular appeal is that they have the self-contained feeling of a complete house.

The design brief for this particular mews was to make optimum use of the available space but, at the same time, retain the individual character of the building. The contrast between the mews and the large Victorian house provided a particularly interesting challenge because you cannot simply transfer an idea that works in one location to another, especially when the scale and spatial quality is so different. The underlying principles and general approach may be the same – even the basic ingredients – but the application must suit the character and proportion of each individual setting.

::

PLANNING THE LAYOUT

When space is limited, the layout is of prime importance. There is a need to make the best use of all that is available – one cannot afford dead corners. Dimensions are critical when the difference between a room that is comfortable and well-organized and one that is an awkward bottleneck may be a matter of inches rather than feet.

Before conversion, the ground floor of this mews was a series of garages, with a single storey above for accommodation. To increase the living area, two garages were turned into a habitable space and another storey was added at the top of the house. Although these changes represented a substantial addition to the total area, the house still retains a period feel. Philip Geraghty was again involved with the planning and coordination of the building work.

Paradoxically, organizing a small space can be easier than planning a larger one. You will probably not need to assess the merits of different layouts because only one will really work. In the case of the mews, the most logical allocation of space was the simplest. Each floor was assigned to a specific activity: the ground floor has become the kitchen/dining room, the first floor is the living room and the rooms on the top storey are bedrooms. Because the entrance to the house is directly off the street, with no mediating strip of garden, a better feeling of space is achieved by locating the living room on the first floor – the views at the upper level extend the area visually without loss of privacy.

THE HALL AND STAIRS

Halls and stairs are more than just connecting spaces. They can be given an identity of their own and, in a small house, if it is not possible to create a view along the hall, attention can be drawn upwards instead.

The stairway in the house, lit from above by a skylight, is painted bright yellow, a positive colour, full of fun, that greets you the moment you step through the front door. Because the expected solution for a small area such as this would be to paint the walls white, this treatment comes as a surprise, creating a lively source of interest that leads the eye upwards and plays down the confined space at the entrance.

As ever, attention to detail is important. The balusters are painted white, but the banister is charcoal grey, matching the skirting boards and adding a crisp, graphic line. At the entrance, black coir runs from wall to wall and from the front door to the bottom stair so that what is only a small floor area is not broken up by different types of flooring. On the first floor landing, double doors open into the living room and the same carpet unifies the two areas. When there is a party, the door can be opened and the landing becomes an extension of the living room.

Right The yellow of the hallway has a glowing impact, and when combined with toplighting from a skylight, this makes a bright and positive treatment for a small area.

THE KITCHEN AND DINING ROOM

Top Bold blind fabric by Howard Hodgkin adds depth to the monochrome scheme.

Above Brightly coloured bowls of fruit contrast with the plain background.

Right The spare, unfussy lines of the dining table and chairs help to maximize space and promote an atmosphere of tranquillity.

On the ground floor, space had to be carefully planned to accommodate both a kitchen and dining area. We wanted to create some kind of separation between the two activities so that guests could be entertained and there would still be a sense of occasion when dining.

The solution was to divide the room with a wall, but to make a large opening in it so that the two areas retain a sense of connection. The opening runs from just below shoulder height up to the ceiling, so the divider is high enough to hide the clutter of cooking, but low enough to function as a bar or raised counter for display.

Another important question was how much space to allocate to the two activities. Because there is no point in having a cramped, awkward dining room, the dining area takes up the greater proportion of available space, and is sufficiently large to allow eight people to be seated comfortably. The kitchen, however, is very compact. With careful planning, it is possible to fit all appliances and storage space you need into quite a small area without sacrificing a sense of scale and space.

The decorative scheme is monochromatic. The walls and door are white, the floor consists of square, pale grey ceramic tiles and the skirting boards are charcoal grey. At the windows, screening the street view, are fine silver Venetian blinds – black would have been too dominant and too dark. To soften their hard edge, there are Roman blinds in a black and white Hodgkin fabric – a bold, painterly design that has great depth and adds interest to the room. The door furniture is chrome and the kitchen counters are terrazzo, a composite of marble chips set in slabs which is strong and durable.

In a small dining room, the dining table takes up a fair proportion of the available space and can look overwhelming. To avoid this and to maximize the feeling of space, a glass-topped table with a simple grey metal frame was chosen.

When a background is plain and simple, accessories play an important role, introducing colour and vitality. Both the table and bar are places where vivid ceramic objects, filled with flowers and fruit, can be arranged. These are easy to move around or replace, adding a dimension of surprise that might otherwise be hard to achieve in such a small area.

THE LIVING ROOM

The living room displays strong contrasting colours and a lively mixture of patterns. But, whereas in my own living room the decoration of the walls matches the furnishing in strength, here the approach was to offset the colours of the fabrics with a monochrome background – white walls and a grey carpet. The carpet, from a Designers Guild range, is neutral – a warm grey with a fine charcoal line running through. To minimize clutter, the whole end wall is given over to storage, with wide shelves flanking the chimney breast and a broad-base shelf accommodating hi-fi equipment and a television.

The decorative scheme is based on two contrasting fabrics. The sofa and upholstered stool are covered with *Moss*, a Hodgkin design in a mixture of greens that has a textural

Below With a wall of shelving to take books, objects and hi-fi equipment, the living room is free of clutter.

quality reminiscent of malachite. Set against this small-scale pattern, two armchairs are covered in the same Hodgkin flower print that is used to upholster the sofa in my living room, but in a different colourway – crimson on black. The injection of red is an important element that prevents the room from having an over-coordinated blue and green look. The large scale of the pattern also helps to increase the sense of space. If a small room is decorated with small coordinating patterns and neutral colours, the result can be both tentative and dull, a constant reminder that space is limited.

It is also important though to know when to stop. There is extensive use of blue in the room to draw the different areas of interest together and provide an underlying harmony, and most of the details and accessories – ceramics, painted tables, cushions, and Roman blinds – although brightly coloured, are plain rather than patterned.

THE MASTER BEDROOM

Because the bedrooms occupy a separate area at the top of the house, they could be decorated in a slightly different way from the other rooms, using light colours and flower prints to promote tranquillity.

The master bedroom is painted in a fresh mint green, which meets the yellow of the hall very happily. *Bourbon Rose*, a print of climbing roses and lilacs, is used to make the Roman blinds and bedcover and to upholster the high headboard, a coordination of surfaces that is soothing rather than overwhelming. Because the pattern is printed on linen, it has a soft, gentle appearance, rather like old chintz. The pale striped fabric on the armchair is complementary in mood rather than sharply contrasting.

The adjoining bathroom is also painted a soft green and half-tiled to match. Even though the room is small, there is a pair of basins, but these are half-basins that project from the wall, a design that is very useful for saving space. Because the side wall is an odd shape, it is completely covered with mirror, a good way of disguising irregularity as well as maximizing light. Since the lavatory occupies a separate area, there is room for a trolley to hold bathroom accessories such as soap, toiletries, face cloths and handtowels.

Above left and top right Pale mint green walls are the background for subtle muted floral prints and an arrangement of Pink Perfection lilies.

Above Black fine metal blinds provide a sharp contrast to the pale green colour scheme of the master bathroom.

THE SECOND BEDROOM

A tiny space, with just enough room for a single bed and a small chest of drawers, the second bedroom has been decorated to create an atmosphere of warmth and intimacy. Peach-painted walls, together with the blond wood of the bureau, make a mellow, enveloping background, counterpointed by the bright green blind. Around the perimeter of the room, a terracotta-and-green wallpaper border, *Graphia*, gives the impression of an architectural detail, while a slightly narrower border is used to outline the angled window reveal.

Although the bed is a simple divan, it has been dressed with piles of plain and patterned cushions to give it the appearance of a daybed. The bedcover is a printed fabric called *Waterlily*, in which all the colours in the room are displayed. On top of the chest of drawers, terracotta ceramics and books, handbound in beautiful marbled papers, add a textural dimension to the overall charm of this room, which lies in the interesting mixture of pattern and colour.

Downstairs is the guest bathroom, containing a shower and a storage area for linen. Again the basin is built-in to maximize floor area and decoration is simple and monochromatic, enlivened by a collection of bright 1930s ceramics.

Above left Warm and mellow, this tiny bedroom is busy with pattern and colour.

Top right A bright green blind covers the recessed window, set off by a vivid and forthright border.

Above The guest bathroom, with fresh flowers and a selection of toiletries.

DESIGNERS GUILD STOCKISTS

All the fabrics, wallpapers, furnishings and accessories in this book are from Designers Guild and may be found in their London Showrooms at 267–277 Kings Road, London SW3 5EN. Designers Guild fabrics and wallpapers are available throughout the UK through a comprehensive network of stockists which includes those listed below.

AVON

Michael Bracey Interiors
30 The Mall, Clifton
Bristol BS8 4DS
Tel: 0272 734664

■

BERKSHIRE

Christine Scott Interiors
50 Northbrook Street
Newbury RG13 1DT
Tel: 0635 551372

■

BUCKINGHAMSHIRE

Morgan Gilder Furnishings
83 High Street
Stony Stratford
Milton Keynes MK11 1AT
Tel: 0908 568674

■

CAMBRIDGESHIRE

At Home
44 Newnham Road
Cambridge CB3 9EY
Tel: 0223 321283

■

CHANNEL ISLANDS

The Designers Choice
21 Seale Street
St Helier
Jersey JE2 3QG
Tel: 0534 24678

J&J Interior Design
Consultants
Glategny Chambers
Glategny Esplanade
St Peter Port
Guernsey GY1 2LP
Tel: 0481 710388

CHESHIRE

Designers
15 London Road
Alderley Edge SK9 7UT
Tel: 0625 586851

■

CORNWALL

Casa Fina Interiors
29 River Street
Truro TR1 2SJ
Tel: 0872 70818

■

DERBYSHIRE

Classic Interiors
6a High Street
Buxton SK17 6EU
Tel: 0298 72063

Interior Design
Matlock Street
Bakewell DE45 1EE
Tel: 0629 813263

■

DEVON

G&H Interiors
1 The Old Pannier Market
High Street
Honiton EX14 8LS
Tel: 0404 42063

■

DORSET

Country Seats
The Square
Beaminster DT8 3AS
Tel: 0308 863545

Individual Interior Design
58–60 Poole Road
Westbourne
Bournemouth BH4 9DZ
Tel: 0202 763256

County Interiors
2 East Borough
Wimborne BH21 1PF
Tel: 0202 880959

■

EIRE

Geraldine Hudson Interiors
2 Herbert Lane
Dublin 2
Tel: 010 353 16600325

ESSEX

Clement Joscelyne Ltd
9–11 High Street
Brentwood CM14 4RG
Tel: 0277 225420

Gillian Anne Designs
30–32 High Road
Buckhurst Hill IG9 5HP
Tel: 081-504 4875/7925

■

GLOUCESTERSHIRE

Jon Edgson Designs &
Decoration
38 Dyer Street
Cirencester GL7 2PF
Tel: 0285 640886

■

GREATER
MANCHESTER

Homes Unlimited
2 Warburton Street
Didsbury Village
Manchester M20 0RA
Tel: 061 434 6278

■

HAMPSHIRE

Pat Staples Interiors
Symes Corner
1 Houchin Street
Bishops Waltham SO3 1AR
Tel: 0489 892626

■

HEREFORD &
WORCESTERSHIRE

John Nash Antiques and
Interiors
Tudor House
17c High Street
Ledbury HR8 1DS
Tel: 0531 635714

■

HERTFORDSHIRE

Clement Joscelyne Ltd
Market Square
Bishop's Stortford CM23 3XA
Tel: 0279 506731

Codicote House Interiors
106 High Street
Codicote
Hitchin SG4 8XE
Tel: 0438 820294

KENT

John Thornton Interiors
43 St Peter's Street
Canterbury CT1 2BG
Tel: 0227 785284

Kent House Sofas
206 Kent House Road
Beckenham BR3 1JN
Tel: 081-778 7782

Kotiki Interiors
22-24 Grove Hill Road
Tunbridge Wells TN1 1RZ
Tel: 0892 521369

Wallpaper World
5 Simpsons Road
Bromley BR2 9AP
Tel: 081-460 9089

■

LANCASHIRE

Campion
24 High Street
Uppermill
Saddleworth
Nr Oldham OL3 6HX
Tel: 0457 876341

Grahams Interiors
402/4 Bolton Road West
Holcombe Brook
Ramsbottom BL0 9RY
Tel: 0204 884911

■

LEICESTERSHIRE

Harlequin Interiors
11 Loseby Lane
Leicester LE1 5DR
Tel: 0533 620994

■

LINCOLNSHIRE

Pilgrim Decor
35 Wide Bargate
Boston PE21 6SR
Tel: 0205 363917

■

LONDON

Baer & Ingram Wallpapers
273 Wandsworth Bridge Road
London SW6 2TX
Tel: 071-736 6111

Harrods
87/135 Brompton Road
Knightsbridge
London SW1X 7XL
Tel: 071-730 1234

Heal & Son
196 Tottenham Court Road
London W1P 9LD
Tel: 071-636 1666

Interiors Of Chiswick
454–458 Chiswick High Road
London W4 5TT
Tel: 081-994 0073

Liberty
Regent Street
London W1 6AH
Tel: 071-734 1234

■

MERSEYSIDE

Judi James Interiors
229 Rose Lane
Allerton
Liverpool L18 5HJ
Tel: 051 724 2956

■

MIDDLESEX

Gallenti
37–39 High Street
Pinner HA5 5PJ
Tel: 081-868 2013

■

NORFOLK

Clement Joscelyne Ltd
The Granary, 5 Bedford Street
Norwich NR2 1AL
Tel: 0603 623220

■

NORTHANTS

Classix
The Old Trinity Church
247 Wellingborough Road
Northampton NN1 4EH
Tel: 0604 232322

■

NORTHERN IRELAND

Fultons Fine Furnishings
55–63 Queen Street
Lurgan BT66 8BN
Tel: 0762 325768

■

NOTTINGHAMSHIRE

Nash Interiors
17–19 Carlton Street
Nottingham NG1 1NL
Tel: 0602 413891

OXON

Pipkins Interiors
68 Church Way
Iffley
Oxford OX4 4EF
Tel: 0865 777147

■

SCOTLAND

Cairns Interiors
111–113 High Street
Old Aberdeen AB2 3EN
Tel: 0224 487490

Decor (Aberdeen) Ltd
157 Skene Street
Aberdeen AB1 1QL
Tel: 0224 646533

Designworks
38 Gibson Street
Glasgow G12 8NX
Tel: 041 339 9520

Mary Maxwell Designs
63 Dublin Street
Edinburgh EH3 6NS
Tel: 031 557 2173

Number Thirty-Five
35 Bridge Street
Dollar
Clacknammanshire FK14 7EZ
Tel: 0259 743339

■

SOMERSET

Paul Carter Interiors
The Studio
Elm House
6 Chip Lane
Taunton TA1 1BZ
Tel: 0823 330404

■

STAFFORDSHIRE

The William Morris Shop
313 Hartshill Road, Hartshill
Stoke-on-Trent ST4 7NR
Tel: 0782 619772

■

SUFFOLK

Clement Joscelyne Ltd
16 Langton Place
Bury St Edmunds IP33 1NE
Tel: 0284 753 824

Edwards of Hadleigh
53 High Street
Hadleigh IP7 5AB
Tel: 0473 827271

SURREY

Katherine Letts Interiors
127 High Street
Godalming GU7 1AF
Tel: 0483 860106

Sage Antiques & Interiors
The Green Cottage
High Street
Ripley GU23 6BB
Tel: 0483 224396

Sue Ralston Designs
8 Station Approach
Kew Gardens
Richmond TW9 3QB
Tel: 081-940 7756

■

SUSSEX

Patricia's of Findon
170 Kings Parade
Findon Road
Findon Valley
West Sussex BN14 OEL
Tel: 0903 692666

Pine & Design Interiors
Haywards Heath Road
Balcombe RH17 2PE
Tel: 0444 811700

Sutton Furnishings
56 Church Road
Hove BN3 2BD
Tel: 0273 723728

The Easy Chair Company
30 Lyndhurst Road
Worthing BN11 2DF
Tel: 0903 201081

■

TYNE & WEAR

Abercrombies
142 Manor House Road
Jesmond
Newcastle Upon Tyne NE2 2NA
Tel: 091 281 7182

Studio Interiors Ltd
4 Old George Yard
Cloth Market
Newcastle Upon Tyne NE1 1EZ
Tel: 091 261 4575

■

WALES

Country Interiors
Goat Street
Haverfordwest
Dyfed SA61 1PX
Tel: 0437 768217

WARWICKSHIRE

Arnold & Bainbridge
30 Smith Street
Warwick CV34 4HS
Tel: 0926 490020

■

WEST MIDLANDS

Bennett & Bowman
Interiors Ltd
4 Beeches Walk
Sutton Coldfield B73 6NN
Tel: 021 354 9371

John Charles Interiors
349 Hagley Road, Edgbaston
Birmingham B17 8DN
Tel: 021 4203977

John Hewins Interiors
1663 High Street, Knowle
Solihull B93 0LL
Tel: 0564 772544

J.W. Treadwell
342–344 Stratford Road
Shirley, Solihull BG0 3DW
Tel: 021 745 3241

■

YORKSHIRE

'Andrena's' Soft
Furnishings & Design
18 Leeds Road
Ilkley LS29 8DJ
Tel: 0943 607185

Cedar House Interiors
7 The Village, Haxby
York YO3 3HS
Tel: 0904 764894

Designer Drapes
217 Bingley Road
Saltaire BD18 4ON
Tel: 0274 593211

Philip Walton
162 Main Street
Addingham
Nr Ilkley LS29 0NA
Tel: 0943 831258

Sue Rugg
Soft Furnishing Design Specialist
11 Eastgate
Bramhope
Leeds LS16 9AT
Tel: 0532 842960

Plaskitt & Plaskitt
8A Walmgate
York YO1 2TJ
Tel: 0904 624670
      0532 432224

ACKNOWLEDGMENTS

DESIGNERS GUILD products are available worldwide through selected representatives in the following countries: Australia, Austria, Belgium & Luxembourg, Cyprus, Denmark, France, Finland, Germany, Greece, Hong Kong, Iceland, Israel, Italy, Japan, Kuwait, Mexico, Netherlands, New Zealand, Norway, Portugal, Saudi Arabia, Singapore, South Africa, Spain, Sweden, Switzerland, Turkey, United Arab Emirates, USA. For further information, please contact Designers Guild at 277 Kings Road, London SW3 5EN Telephone 071-351 5775 Fax 071-352 7258.

Michael Boys 20; Linda Burgess/Insight 11 below, 12 above right, 13 centre left, 15 above left, 15 centre left, 16–17 centre; Michelle Garrett/Insight; Gazuit/Agence Top 15 centre right; Jerry Harpur 13 below left; Marijke Heuff 13 above right; Pierre Hussenot/Agence Top 13 bottom left; Guy Marineau/ Agence Top 16–17 below; Carlos Navajas 10 below, 11 above, 11 centre, 12 centre right, 12 below left, 12 bottom left, 12 bottom right, 13 below right, 13 bottom right, 15 above right, 15 bottom left; Perdereau-Thomas 10 above, 10 centre, 11 above left, 12 above left, 12 centre left, 12 below right, 13 centre right, 15 below right, 15 bottom right; Laurent Rosseau/Agence Top 15 below left; Brian E Rybolt/Impact Photos 13 above left; The Tate Gallery, London 11 bottom right; Trustees of the Victoria & Albert Museum 11 centre left, 11 bottom left.

AUTHOR'S ACKNOWLEDGMENTS

I am truly grateful to all those who have devoted so much skill, energy, commitment and generosity of spirit to make this book possible. In particular I would like to thank Jo Willer, Evelyn Shearer, Andy Luckett and the team at Designers Guild, Simon and Nicky Jeffreys for letting us photograph the mews house, and all those whose work is represented in the book: Jake Aitken, Pierre Beaudry, Janet and Paul Czainski, Adrian Everitt, Kaffe Fassett, Philip Geraghty, Michael Heindorf, Liz Hodges, Howard Hodgkin, Bill Jacklin, Bernard Jacobsen, Brian Johnson, Bruce McLean, Carol McNichol, Roger Oates, Janice Tchalenko, William Tillyer, Richard Womersley.

INDEX